Grace by which I Stand

Lin Lockamy

WestBow Press
A DIVISION OF THOMAS NELSON
& ZONDERVAN

Copyright © 2014 Lin Lockamy.

All rights reserved. No part of this book may be used or reproduced by any means, graphic, electronic, or mechanical, including photocopying, recording, taping or by any information storage retrieval system without the written permission of the publisher except in the case of brief quotations embodied in critical articles and reviews.

WestBow Press books may be ordered through booksellers or by contacting:

WestBow Press
A Division of Thomas Nelson & Zondervan
1663 Liberty Drive
Bloomington, IN 47403
www.westbowpress.com
1 (866) 928-1240

Because of the dynamic nature of the Internet, any web addresses or links contained in this book may have changed since publication and may no longer be valid. The views expressed in this work are solely those of the author and do not necessarily reflect the views of the publisher, and the publisher hereby disclaims any responsibility for them.

Any people depicted in stock imagery provided by Thinkstock are models, and such images are being used for illustrative purposes only. Certain stock imagery © Thinkstock.

ISBN: 978-1-4908-5576-9 (sc)
ISBN: 978-1-4908-5575-2 (hc)
ISBN: 978-1-4908-5577-6 (e)

Library of Congress Control Number: 2014918035

Printed in the United States of America.

WestBow Press rev. date: 11/03/2014

DEDICATION

Pain is inevitable; joy is optional...

    Although the physical pain was overwhelming at times, Kami and Trey, you are and forever will be my true joy. You were both there every step of the way. It is my honor to be called your mom. Thank you for sharing the tears and laughter. As our journey continues, our faith in God strengthens.

                  I love you both.
                      -Mom

CONTENTS

Acknowledgments ix
Introduction: After the Sirens xi

1. The Choices We Make 1
2. The Rescue 19
3. Help Arrives with Precise Timing 35
4. You Never Know When 53
5. The Weight We Carry 69
6. Reconstruction—New Creation 89
7. A Glimpse of What Awaits 101
8. Moment to Moment 113
9. Glory to Glory 121

God's Grace Continues 131

ACKNOWLEDGMENTS

I can't even begin to thank the scores of people who prayed for my family and me during and after the horrific accident. I do want everyone to know that no matter how physically and emotionally painful this could have been, we chose to see God's hand through it all and did not suffer as you would imagine. God IS good.

Thank you to my first responders, who consisted of several teams of firefighters, paramedics, and police who were on the scene. Many members of my church, St. Dunstan's Episcopal Church in Houston, were at the scene as well. They sent out prayer requests that spanned the country by nightfall. To these and all who have sent up prayers on our behalf, I give my heartfelt thanks to you.

Numerous individuals helped along the way in various ways. Thanks to Bilinda, who was at my bedside, prayed with me, and watched over my children when I could not; to Matt, who endured the uncertainties, shared in each small stride, and weathered the years that followed; and to Pat, my loving sister, who took on each and every role of setting up our new life. I felt the comfort of the prayers from my church and many others. Thank you.

I am grateful to David and especially acknowledge his incredible dedication and unceasing determination to release my ankle from the wreckage. Because of his tenacity, I have legs.

Many others shared this journey with me. I am grateful to each and every one, named and unnamed. Some of the many include Kathie, Monica, Father Rob, Peggy, Jeri, Bob, Janice, June, Renee, Lynn, Dallas, and the Angel on the Plane.

To Art, whose photograph on the cover is breathtaking, thank you for allowing me to share it. Your enthusiasm to shoot the photo on the back cover is the icing on the cake. It has been my honor to work with you.

To Judy Armstrong, my editor, who poured over this manuscript for hours on end, what an amazing job you did. Thank you for being part of this journey with me.

To Mom and Dad, thank you for instilling the foundation of faith that forever grows in me. I can't wait until we meet again.

But most of all, I thank God for the blessings He bestows upon each and every one of us. May He continue to guide this journey to what awaits!

INTRODUCTION

AFTER THE SIRENS

We all react when we hear sirens. In fact, we react with heart-pounding urgency whenever we hear siren after siren. Some of us even take a moment to pray for those who are in need as well as for the first responders.

On *that day*, police cars, fire trucks, EMTs, and ambulances kept coming. Although it was close to time for a shift change, the first responders to arrive stayed on to assist those who came on duty later. Already, they were part of all that happened *that day*.

Passersby, who paused to stare at the tangled mess of metal and machine, wondered how this could have happened.

That morning, I was up and working early. My son, Trey, needed a ride to get to school early for some help. I threw on my favorite gray sweat pants and T-shirt, grabbed my purse and keys, and, for some reason, decided to put on my new diamond tennis bracelet—a gift from my husband. It was a gift that I would never see again after *that day*. I dropped Trey off at school and headed home—or so I thought. There was a light but continuous drizzle that morning, and I noticed the streets were somewhat slick and slippery as I stopped at a traffic signal. When the light turned green, I accelerated slowly because of the slippery feel of the road. I remember a dark-colored pickup truck coming toward me. I watched as its front wheels crossed the yellow lines on the road, heading into my lane. I distinctly remember thinking, *He's out of control.*

The truck hit my SUV head-on but slightly off center, forcing us to collide a second time. The rate of speed and impact of the truck, which was slightly lower than my SUV, caused the truck to slide under the front end of my Expedition, sending it airborne. It twisted 180 degrees in midair and landed on top of another Expedition that had been beside me, crushing it completely. The two white Expeditions, now entangled, were careening forward, out of control, for almost a block. When the tangled wreckage finally came to a stop, my car overturned and hit a brick wall, causing it to tumble down.

A video from a local business captured the initial impact. The indescribable sound of an enormous explosion, with spectacular flashes of light splitting the wreckage while dust and debris flew in all directions, was heart-stopping to watch. In the video footage, it was difficult to determine which car was which. When the dust settled, three vehicles in all—a pickup truck and two white Expeditions—lay in ruins. Bits of metal, glass, rubber, and other assorted car parts lay scattered across the pavement, covering the road as far as one could see. The street lay still, as every motorist stopped in fearful awe of what was happening. An eerie silence fell upon the whole scene—and then the sirens began.

1

THE CHOICES WE MAKE

Pain is inevitable but misery is optional.
We cannot avoid pain,
but we can avoid joy.
~Tim Hansel

As a parent who was involved in my children's lives, I was keenly aware that I was really not in charge of much of anything at all—at least, that's what I thought. In fact, it was my responsibility to keep myself spiritually focused, but I had made no conscious effort to do so. At the time of the accident, I couldn't have imagined that there were lots—and I do mean *lots*—of people praying for me and for my family.

We have all seen TV medical dramas that show trauma patients as they slowly start to become aware of their surroundings, and images begin to appear through the hazy fog of semi consciousness. Well, for me, this was no TV drama—it was real, and one of those hazy images turned out to be my friend Bilinda, to whom I had entrusted the care of my children. Bilinda was at my bedside, saying, "Do you know you were on prayer chains even while you were still trapped in the wreckage? And by that night, those prayer chains had been extended nationwide!" Her words instantly comforted me.

Every day, Bilinda came to the hospital, read Scripture, and prayed with me, and somehow I knew everything would be okay, whatever that meant. I tried to take things a moment at a time, and that was a conscious decision. I could not handle more than that, but looking back, I can see that the path was clear and calm right from the accident scene. Now I see and can share that I did not suffer in the way one might think. I kept telling people this, but it took time—God's time—to see this more clearly. And He has given me the words to explain the awesome lessons I am now ready to share with you. Other people from church told me they put me on prayer chains at many other churches. So that night, March 28, 2006, I was on prayer chains across the country. What could be more comforting than that? Since then, several of those churches have called for updates. Wow!

We make choices regarding how to handle almost everything. We choose to have a positive attitude. We choose to put our faith in God and try to live our lives knowing He will be there through it all. I knew in my heart that I would walk someday. I told everybody that, and everyone would immediately check my meds. You see, the doctors knew, without any discussion, I would not be able to walk again—not with these legs. But I knew I would! I was not sure whether I would walk on my own legs or with some type of assistance, but I knew I would be walking again someday. So I chose not to focus on the "uglies," as I often referred to them. I knew I would walk again someday and chose not to dwell on what I might have to go through in the meantime.

After years of hearing people tell me that I had a wonderful attitude and would be ministering to those who came to minister to me, I am now beginning to see how basic it is to make the choice each day to live by faith in God. I guess I knew that, but I could never seem to grasp that walking in faith is a choice. It is, and it needs to become the basic foundation of life. I had never really thought about it that way before the accident.

I was brought up Catholic and went to church, studied my catechism, and went to a private Catholic school through eighth grade. Church was a part of my life but not really life itself. It was not until I was a little older and began to seek out other churches that I had a desire to apply what God has called us to do: *live* my faith. Having children and wanting to bring them up in a family in which faith was a conscious decision was my plan, but of course, it was God who led the way.

Much to my surprise, it was the accident (which I often refer to as the "blow to the head") that led to this realization. I'm sure you've heard that sometimes it takes a direct hit, an unmistakable action, for some people to "get it." Well, my accident was that direct hit for me. Once my life settled into a post-hospital routine, it seemed like music entered my life again. Music was absent during the hospital stay and the daily effort to function. I had forgotten how much music lifts me out of the chaos of life.

One particular song played frequently during that time. It was new to me, but every time I heard it, I felt intensely moved. The problem was that I could never remember the name of the song or who sang it. Eventually, I realized I could remember the name of the group who sang it by associating their name with the car I drove: Avalon. My kids were thrilled to finally be able to narrow the search for the song. As it turned out, it was actually an old song: "Testify to Love." The words lightened my heart, and I loved the melody and the passion that I heard in their rendition, yet there was something else staring me in the face. Because I grew up in the Catholic Church, the words *testify* and *witness* were not exactly words I felt comfortable with. That was for other people. Those were not things I envisioned myself doing. But I related to this song so strongly that I felt compelled to embrace these words.

This song still touches me so deeply that I have redefined the words *testify* and *witness*. I am not a Bible scholar; in fact, the more I read and study the Bible, the more infantile I feel. I am a novice. But I have become passionate about sharing how God has shown me to keep an open mind and open heart and learn to see His blessings in everything. This attitude is the way in which to live. Like everyone, I am not perfect at this lifestyle, but it's something to work toward. It is rewarding to receive a second chance and to have people relate to my experiences and want to know more. This is incredible to me! So I keep sharing, and I also try to remember to thank those who touch me. This is my new definition of what it means to testify and witness: to share God's love through words of encouragement and through stories of His miracles, calling attention to His blessings and the beauty around us.

I had the opportunity to meet one of the singers in Avalon, Greg Long, and I shared with him that his song "Testify to Love" was and is an inspiration to me. I got to thank him in person. It was my intention to share with him just how much the song inspired me as I began to recover from the accident. He seemed to understand.

Several months later, Reid, a friend of mine who plays in a contemporary band at his church sent me a song. It was a new song, and they were going to play it the following Sunday. He thought the song might be especially meaningful to me. It was entitled "Bless the Broken Road". It is a beautiful song, but when I got up the next morning, I felt angry. I might not have all the abilities I had before the accident, but I don't feel that life is a struggle, as this song seemed to imply. I decided to send Reid a clip of my favorite song, my inspiration and the way I want to live. I searched online to find "Testify to Love." The first recording I found was not by Avalon, so I was going to try again, but I listened to this first result anyway. It was a clip of Wynona Judd singing on the TV show *Touched by an Angel*. It was the same song yet so much more. In the show, there was a large gathering of people who were singing with all their passion. Then the camera panned over to a little boy who was obviously dying. He was in a wheelchair, so I was a bit taken aback, until I saw that he was sitting on a handmade quilt eerily similar to mine, made for me by the ladies from St. Dunstan's. By now, you can assume I was an emotional mess. I sent this entire story back to Reid with the link to the video I'd found. He too was speechless. God can touch you anywhere at any time if you choose to look and listen.

Shortly thereafter, I had the opportunity to meet Janna Long of Avalon. I shared this story with her. She remembered the clip and was also touched, and she called Greg over so that I could share it with him. Not long after that, I had the opportunity to meet the remaining members of Avalon. Greg was so excited that he asked me to share my story with the other two members of the group. I wasn't sure where to start. Then Greg said, "Tell them about the video." So due to my friend's desire to share a great song with me, I was encouraged to share my song of inspiration with him, and the story grew from there. Choose to share. Choose to pass on God's blessings. What a great choice it is!

Recently, I had lunch with a business associate so that she could introduce me to someone on her staff. Women naturally have chats from the heart, and these ladies asked to hear more about the accident and the blessings I saw through it all. We ended up diving right into a discussion of the mom struggles rather than the physical challenges. That night, I received an e-mail from the lady I had just met. She has three young children and is no doubt a dedicated mom. She thanked me for meeting with her that day. She wanted me to know that when she'd gotten home from that meeting, she had taken a moment to just stand and watch her family with an awareness of how thankful she was for each of her children and her husband. She took the time to recognize and appreciate all that God had blessed her with—and then she shared it with me. Choose to take the time to soak in blessings that you might otherwise take for granted.

It might take hearing or reading of a tragedy or difficulty in someone else's life to get our attention, but it's our choice to recognize the gifts we have and to thank God that we can appreciate all He has given us. To share that moment of utter gratitude with others makes it even better!

After I learned to walk again, I started a completely different regimen of physical therapy. I met lots of people who were recovering from all kinds of injuries and who needed rehabilitation. Most of them were working to recover from surgeries. One woman next to me seemed tired and weary. She stopped to ask me what I was recovering from. I gave her the quick overview: I was in an accident, my car overturned and trapped me, and the rescue teams were going to take my legs to get me out but did not have to. I'm sure I looked like a little tyke just learning to walk and beaming with pride. She seemed stunned. She proceeded to tell me about her best friend, whom she had lost recently in a car accident. Her friend's car had overturned and trapped her, but the rescue teams *had* taken her legs to get to her—and then they'd lost her. I was silent. I had heard about this accident. It had occurred shortly after my own and not far from the location of my accident. At that moment, I came face-to-face with the reality of two similar accidents with two different outcomes. There I stood, blessed to have survived. Then I became a little concerned that this lady might feel some anger that I had survived and her friend had not. Rather than becoming angry, we shared a private moment. We both realized it was God's plan for us to meet that day. We sat in awe of God's amazing works. Somehow, my being there and working hard to regain mobility gave her a sense of peace and restoration that although God allows bad things to happen, His light can radiate through others. She chose to see how great God's grace is, even though neither of us understood why He chose to take her friend and not me. I left with an even greater sense of gratitude that God kept me on this earth and has a purpose for my life.

While I was in the hospital, my daughter came in one day, laughing. She thought Mr. Doyle was hysterical. He is a friend who owns a local restaurant. Apparently, he had sent enough food to the house to feed the whole neighborhood! In my daughter, I saw a precious young girl laugh and be just that—a young girl—rather than someone now trying to take on the parental role, overwhelmed with stress. Her smile and delight in Mr. Doyle's gesture forever touched me. By the way, they froze some of that food because there was so much of it, so I got to have some when I was finally able to go home—and it was wonderful! Even more wonderful for me was the reminder that my daughter had at least one moment of relief from the nightmare she was living. Later, I had the opportunity to share this story with Mr. Doyle. He felt as we often do, as if he couldn't do enough to make a situation better. As it turned out, he did far more than feeding the neighborhood. We never know whom our seemingly small gestures might touch. We need to make the choice to do whatever we can and let God unveil the rest.

I had been walking for about a year, when a youth group from my church asked me to go on a mission trip. I was one of the adult sponsors. Bilinda was with me. There is no doubt God had once again put her there as my angel, to watch out for me as I attempted to be a part of this effort with the kids. It was a fabulous trip to Mississippi to assist in the rebuilding effort in the area devastated by Hurricane Katrina.

As I arrived and readied my bunk—which, by the way, was the top bunk, since that was all that was left—Bilinda reminded me that I should not be climbing. The other adults inquired and offered to help. I explained that I had been in an accident that had crushed my legs but that the fact that I was still here and could walk made for a great life! One woman seemed a little more intrigued than most of the others. She sat beside me as they all gathered around, asking questions with genuine concern. I love being in these moments, when I'm given the opportunity to share the story of God's love and protection, and the lessons He has taught me become so apparent for all to see. If I can be a vessel for God's glory, that's okay with me! This woman didn't waste any time in telling me I should write a book. That wasn't the first time I had heard those words—the suggestion had started with Bilinda while I was still lying in the hospital. Why on earth would I ever want to write a book, much less a book about the accident? It wasn't long before I too understood that if I was to follow God's rather obvious plan, I was supposed to write and share what He allowed me to understand. But you know, I can still hear her voice and see that she meant this in a way few others had. We didn't get a chance to sit down together that week, because we had a busy but fun-filled week with the kids. It weighed on my heart that I wanted to talk with her. Who was she? And why was she so intrigued by the fact that I could see God's blessings through this accident?

As we were loading up the vans and saying our good-byes, I wished I could see this woman again. I wanted to stay in touch with her, but I didn't even know her name. The night before we were to leave, we had a wonderful service on the beach. The moon was bright, there was live guitar music, and everyone was singing in such majesty—it was a truly awesome moment! Suddenly, I realized the woman was there. In fact, she was the deacon leading the service that night. The site of her took my breath away. I knew at that moment that I was, in fact, supposed to write and continue on this new path. I'll say it once again: you never know whom you might touch or whom God will put in your path, but when God gives you all the pieces of the puzzle, boy, is it awesome—and you must make that choice to listen to Him and follow.

Throughout many of the months following the accident, I was not conscious of making choices of faith or choosing to have a positive attitude. Now I look at that as a blessing. I didn't struggle with decisions. God gave me peace and direction—and I wasn't even paying attention. Fortunately, when we pause to look back, we can catch the lessons we missed at the time. My choice was to give God control and follow where He leads.

My daughter, Kami, who was eighteen and a senior in high school at the time of the accident, was busy and stressed with her own position in life. The thought of losing her mother at eighteen and feeling as if she needed to run the household and be a mom to her younger brother was overwhelming. I could see that. A few days after I came home, my sister, Pat, came from New York to help establish a routine with the kids and the house and to get me on a schedule and hire a nurse. That was part of my discharge promise: I could not be left alone—ever. Pat had things under way quickly. She asked me what I needed. Without a doubt, my need was to see my daughter return to the life of an eighteen-year-old getting ready to graduate. I couldn't bear to see the stress in her eyes anymore, so I asked my sister to take my daughter shopping—anywhere—so that she could go out and have some fun. That would be the best medicine for me. And that was what she did. They shopped and had a few hours away from the atmosphere of upheaval and uncertainty at home. I knew Pat had achieved my hope of a fun day for my daughter when Kami skipped into my bedroom, holding a huge stuffed flower. I still have it on my bed to this day. My sister chose to honor my wishes. As a mom, she knew that the best thing she could do for me was to relieve the stress from Kami for a while. And so it was—a choice and a gift I will never forget.

As time passed and my sister left, Kami once again bore the burden of playing the roles of mom and caretaker. I laugh every time I think of this—she sat me down to have a talk. Remember, I was in a wheelchair, possibly for life, but what a scene it was! Kami was in my face, asking me why I wasn't taking the doctor's prognosis of never walking again seriously. She felt I was missing the enormity of the situation. I, on the other hand, chose not to waste my time worrying about the medical prognosis. I questioned her instead. What did she think I was supposed to be doing? Was I to sit and cry for what abilities I had lost? I choose not to cry. I choose to share in the joy of what one little thing I could do that day. I could lower my legs—sometimes. This development was huge progress! I could lift my own legs—at times; I was becoming more proficient at moving in and out of my wheelchair and the car. I told her that I was keenly aware that at forty-seven, I could not move by myself. I was completely and utterly dependent on someone else for everything. I understood exactly where I was. Kami realized that day that she could let go of some of the burden she was carrying. Mom was still right there. Although somewhat incapacitated, her mom had not changed. I didn't have on rose-colored glasses. I knew the score well. I chose not to let it get me down and encouraged both my children to share in the laughter as I learned to do everyday things again. And laugh we did!

We later ran into this issue again (those words—*ran into*—bring an uneasy smile!). We came across a time when my home physical therapist asked me to stand on both legs. They were still badly broken, but she felt that my body weight might help stimulate the bone growth. It took the physical therapist, my nurse, and my daughter to stand me up. But I was up! It was such a strange feeling. The physical therapist suggested that the doctor might let me begin to walk with boots on to stimulate the bone growth since there was little sign of the bones healing. This was not a good sign. Although the legs appeared to be healing on the outside, the inside was an entirely different story. If the bones didn't begin to heal soon, the doctors may be forced to amputate my legs. I was by no means out of the woods yet.

I felt in my heart there was no way my doctor would entertain the idea of my walking, but I felt hopeful about having this conversation at my next doctor's appointment. Of course, I shared this hope with everyone who would listen. My daughter once again felt the need to help me return to reality. She sat me down again and explained that there was no way the orthopedic surgeon was going to allow me to walk—with or without boots—at this point. Once again, I assured her that I knew that but thought it was fun to have a goal. And who knew? Maybe it would happen someday. And it did! Not then, but months later.

First, the doctor allowed me to walk on my right leg, and then, eventually, I began to put some weight on the left with a boot on. I choose to look forward. Yes, there were moments filled with tears for the uncertainty ahead, but I always remembered that I was in God's hands and that He had plans for me. I prayed that I would be able to understand why He had let me live. What was I supposed to do? I struggled with explaining to people that discovering God's purpose for my life was now my passion. While listening to a local Christian radio station, I heard Mary Beth Chapman being interviewed sometime after her children had been involved in an accident in which she had lost a young daughter. The interviewer asked her if she ever wondered why God had allowed that to happen. She instantly replied, "No, I only hope I steward this message well." Awesome! Those were the words I had so desperately been searching for. Rather than getting caught up in why, she and I were blessed to immediately feel comfort in the knowledge that God has a plan and that it is up to us to listen and allow His plan to unfold through sharing His blessings and grace with others. And He has!

Let's look at this same lesson in Scripture. Over and over, Jesus gives us examples of ordinary men and women who choose to trust in Him. Some triumph immediately; some don't see the rewards until much later. But make no mistake—we make the choice to trust in the Lord over and over again.

> *When he had finished speaking, he said to Simon, "Put out into deep water, and let down the nets for a catch."*
>
> *Simon answered, "Master, we've worked hard all night and haven't caught anything. But because you say so, I will let down the nets."*

> When they had done so, they caught such a large number of fish that their nets began to break. So they signaled their partners in the other boat to come and help them, and they came and filled both boats so full that they began to sink.
>
> When Simon Peter saw this, he fell at Jesus' knees and said, "Go away from me, Lord; I am a sinful man!" For he and all his companions were astonished at the catch of fish they had taken, and so were James and John, the sons of Zebedee, Simon's partners.
>
> Then Jesus said to Simon, "Don't be afraid; from now on you will catch men."
>
> So they pulled their boats up on shore, left everything and followed him. Luke 5:4–11 (NIV)

I would say this message is pretty straightforward. Jesus requested. Simon obeyed even though he did not agree, and immediately, Jesus delivered an amazing catch. Yet Jesus had taught them much more than just how to catch fish in this lesson.

> David said to Saul, "Let no one lose heart on account of this Philistine; your servant will go and fight him."
>
> Saul replied, "You are not able to go out against this Philistine and fight him; you are only a boy and he has been a fighting man from his youth."
>
> But David said to Saul, "Your servant has been keeping his father's sheep. When a lion or bear came and carried off a sheep from the flock, I went after it, struck it and rescued the sheep from its mouth. When it turned to me, I seized it by its hair, struck it and killed it. Your servant has killed

both the lion and the bear; this uncircumcised Philistine will be like one of them, because he has defied the armies of the living God. The Lord who delivered me from the paw of the lion and the paw of the bear will deliver me from the hand of the Philistine."

Saul said to David, "Go, and the LORD be with you."

Then Saul dressed David in his own tunic. He put a coat of armor on him and a bronze helmet on his head. David fastened on his sword over the tunic and tried walking around, because he was not used to them.

"I cannot go in these," he said to Saul, "because I am not used to them." So he took them off. Then he took his staff in his hand, chose five smooth stones from the stream, put them in the pouch of his shepherd's bag and, with his sling in his hand, approached the Philistine.

Meanwhile, the Philistine, with his shield bearer in front of him, kept coming closer to David. He looked David over and saw that he was only a boy, ruddy and handsome, and he despised him. He said to David, "Am I a dog, that you come at me with sticks?" And the Philistine cursed David by his gods. "Come here," he said, "and I'll give your flesh to the birds of the air and the beasts of the field!"

David said to the Philistine, "You come against me with sword and spear and javelin, but I come against you in the name of the Lord Almighty, the God of the armies of Israel, whom you have defied. This day the Lord will hand you over to me, and I'll strike you down and cut off your head. Today I will give the carcasses of the Philistine army to the birds of the air and the beasts of the earth, and the whole world

> *will know that there is a God in Israel. All those gathered here will know that it is not by sword or spear that the Lord saves; for the battle is the Lord's and he will give all of you into our hands."*
>
> *As the Philistine moved closer to attack him, David ran quickly toward the battle line to meet him. Reaching into his bag and taking out a stone, he slung it and struck the Philistine on the forehead. The stone sank into his forehead, and he fell face down on the ground.*
>
> *So David triumphed over the Philistine with a sling and a stone; without a sword in his hand he struck down the Philistine and killed him.* 1 Samuel 17:32–50 (NIV)

We might not see anything like this literal sword-versus-stone experience in our lifetime, but as we look back over those times when we allowed God to guide us into the work He has called us to do, we will see that He has provided us with the exact equipment we needed to overcome against some "giant" odds.

> *When Jesus heard what had happened, he withdrew by boat privately to a solitary place. Hearing of this, the crowds followed him on foot from the towns. When Jesus landed and saw a large crowd, he had compassion on them and healed their sick.*
>
> *As evening approached, the disciples came to him and said, "This is a remote place, and it's already getting late. Send the crowds away, so they can go to the villages and buy themselves some food."*
>
> *Jesus replied, "They do not need to go away. You give them something to eat."*

> "We have here only five loaves of bread and two fish," they answered.
>
> "Bring them here to me," he said. And he directed the people to sit down on the grass. Taking the five loaves and the two fish and looking up to heaven, he gave thanks and broke the loaves. Then he gave them to the disciples, and the disciples gave them to the people. They all ate and were satisfied, and the disciples picked up twelve basketfuls of broken pieces that were left over. The number of those who ate was about five thousand men, besides women and children.
> Matthew 14:13–21 (NIV)

Jesus performed many miracles. He healed many and fed thousands with little. Although those miracles were great in magnitude, the miracles He performs in your life and mine are even greater!

> *Jesus continued: "There was a man who had two sons. The younger one said to his father, 'Father, give me my share of the estate,' so he divided his property between them.*
>
> *"Not long after that, the younger son got together all he had, set off for a distant country and there squandered his wealth in wild living. After he had spent everything, there was a severe famine in that whole country, and he began to be in need. So he went and hired himself out to a citizen of that country, who sent him to his fields to feed pigs. He longed to fill his stomach with the pods that the pigs were eating, but no one gave him anything.*
>
> *"When he came to his senses, he said, 'How many of my father's hired men have food to spare, and here I am starving to death! I will set out and go back to my father and say to*

him: Father, I have sinned against heaven and against you. I am no longer worthy to be called your son; make me like one of your hired men.' So he got up and sent to his father.

"But while he was a long way off, his father saw him and was filled with compassion for him; he ran to his son, threw his arms around him and kissed him.

"The son said to him, 'Father, I have sinned against heaven and against you. I am no longer worthy to be called your son.'

"But the father said to his servants, 'Quick! Bring the best robe and put it on him. Put a ring on his finger and sandals on his feet. Bring the fattened calf and kill it. Let's have a feast and celebrate. For this son of mine was dead and is alive again; he was lost and is found.' So they began to celebrate.

"Meanwhile the older son was in the field. When he came near the house, he heard music and dancing. So he called one of the servants and asked him what was going on. 'Your brother has come,' he replied, 'and your father has killed the fattened calf because he has him back safe and sound.'

"The older brother became angry and refused to go in. So his father went out and pleaded with him. But he answered his father, 'Look! All these years I've been slaving for you and never disobeyed your orders. Yet you never gave me even a young goat so I could celebrate with my friends. But when this son of yours who has squandered your property with prostitutes comes home, you kill the fattened calf for him!'

"'My son,' the father said, 'you are always with me, and everything I have is yours. But we had to celebrate and be *glad, because this brother of yours was dead and is alive again; he was lost and is found.'"* Luke 15:11–32 (NIV)

This is a story most of us have heard. Many have studied the lessons of forgiveness as the son sees the error of his ways and returns to his father not as the son of privilege he once was but as a servant. The father forgives the son, who has made some bad choices. They both choose forgiveness. They make choices. Recently, I read a deep commentary on this parable: *The Prodigal Son*, by Timothy Keller.

Jesus doesn't tell us the end of the story. Interesting! Could it be that he wants us to think this through for ourselves and see more than what we all initially saw in the parable?

We don't seem to give much thought to the choice the older brother made to ignore or disown his younger brother. In the story, he chooses to hang on to the anger toward his brother's squandered inheritance and whatever effects his brother might have had on his own inheritance. Surely, this is not what God would want us to focus on.

Once again, Jesus told a story for us to ponder, learn, and carry out.

2

THE RESCUE

"So I have come down to rescue them"
~Exodus 3:8 (NIV)

The story of my rescue from the car is not mine alone but that of many. The firefighters and paramedics worked together to rescue me from the car. I'll take you through many facets of my rescue from that day forward.

The firefighters and paramedics were called to a horrific scene: two Expeditions and a truck, all completely demolished, each with a single occupant. My Expedition had been hit head-on in such a way as to cause a second collision with that same truck, sending my car airborne. My vehicle twisted 180 degrees and then landed on top of the second Expedition. Then it overturned into a brick wall. Fortunately, the drivers of the other two vehicles were easily accessible to extricate from the wreckage, though they were critically injured. A team of paramedics was attending each driver in an effort to stabilize them so that they could be transported with the utmost care and speed.

On the other hand, I was trapped. The airbags deployed, buckled inward, and my Expedition was lying on its side in a pile of broken glass on the ground. The dashboard pinned both of my legs and crushed them. This presented a challenge for firefighters and paramedics extricating me from the car. They cut off the roof of the car, but the car was too close to the brick wall to get any machinery in to assist in moving it out of the way or even to create enough space to facilitate anyone getting inside the car to work from there. As the firefighters considered turning my Expedition back to its upright position, the paramedics said they feared such a move might compound my injuries or potentially be fatal. They were particularly concerned about the possibility of neck injuries. After much discussion between the two groups, they came up with a possible solution. Although pinned, I remained conscious and was able to talk to one of the firefighters. He asked me if I could move my right ankle. I could not. They now faced another obstacle in the rescue effort. There was something other than the dashboard pinning my ankle. Uncertain as to what was keeping the ankle stuck, they had to come up with a different way to get me out to avoid further injury to the ankle.

These highly trained teams called for the Jaws of Life, a machine that can cut through anything. Mysteriously, it made no impact on the wreckage at all. Believing the machine was not functioning properly, they quickly arranged for a second Jaws of Life to be brought to the scene immediately. All the while, the paramedics were watching the clock. As a matter of procedure, they wanted me out and my injuries assessed at the one-hour mark. The second Jaws of Life arrived but also did no good. The machine had no effect whatsoever on the car. The firefighters and paramedics had to determine how to get me out quickly, as time was running out. The reality was that no technique they had been trained to use was working in this set of circumstances. I remember hearing these words over and over again: "We're running out of time." Even though I was in and out of consciousness, I heard them explaining just what that meant. If "time ran out," they were going to take my legs in order to free me from the car in the hope of saving my life. I could hear the frustration in their voices. I knew they were doing all they possibly could to get me out in one piece.

Later in this chapter, I will explain how God was at work there, even while I was still trapped in the wreckage. It took months before I was able to see how the whole story was revealed. A man named David was the firefighter who was by my side the entire time. His goal was to release the right ankle. He could not bear to see them take my legs. He was not ready to give up! Later, he told me he yelled to his partner, who was at the underside of the engine, "Grab a crowbar, and just start moving anything you can." David was still next to me, down by my ankle, with no room to move, trying to see if there was any sign that the metal was giving as his partner diligently worked with the crowbar. There was a slight indication that the metal moved! David screamed to his partner to continue to work on that particular spot. They managed to move the metal just enough to release the ankle and then lifted the dashboard off my legs and slid me out through the back of the car. Within minutes, they had hoisted me onto a gurney, and a team of paramedics sprang into action.

The paramedics did all they could to assess the injuries and stabilize me so that I could be loaded into the Life Flight helicopter, which had been waiting on the scene during the entire ordeal. As the Life Flight crew carried me toward the red helicopter, Father Rob stopped them and requested they allow him, my husband, and a friend to have a moment of prayer with me. The training of the Life Flight crew includes a warning that time is of the essence and that every moment counts. Since they were nearing the critical hour-and-a-half post-trauma mark, they could not stop their mission for prayer time. Father Rob later told me that there were several conversations before the Life Flight crew agreed to pause long enough to allow them to pray with me. I remember opening my eyes and seeing Rob smiling at me. At that moment, I didn't see him as a priest who had been called to administer last rites; he was simply my smiling friend. He gave me a small black rope tied in a circle—a prayer rope, something I could hold on to as we prayed. I kept it with me in the hospital, and it went home with me later, where it remains to this day.

I opened my eyes a second time and saw my husband. He was smiling too, but his was a nervous, worried smile. I seemed to hear a voice saying, "Tell him you love him first; you may not get a second chance." So I told him, "I love you; my legs are killing me, but I'll be fine." It wasn't until years later that I began to ponder what the voice had told me.

I remember a sound like a ping—like metal against metal. I knew exactly what it was. It was the gurney coming into contact with the helicopter as I was being loaded. Other than that sound, I don't remember anything of my first helicopter ride.

The accident victims weren't the only ones who needed rescuing that morning. My daughter eventually shared with me what she was experiencing during that time. Kami was driving to school, just as she did every weekday morning. Traffic began to slow. She could see that there had been a horrible accident. She immediately saw the overturned white Expedition, which was the same color as mine. She thought the person in that car must surely have died. Kami was a senior in high school. She was in training to become an EMT and thought maybe she should get out to see if she might be of assistance, but there were already many people flocking to each of the three vehicles to assist, so she decided it might not be a good idea. Besides, she knew she would not be allowed to assist a family member. What a haunting thought for a young teen! She was on her way to the local Walgreen's to observe the pharmacist that day as part of her training. The students had been instructed to treat these assignments like real jobs. They needed to be on time, and since she had been detained, she picked up her cell phone to call her teacher to say there had been a terrible accident on the way to school that might cause her to be late. She was the last car allowed to pass the scene. The cars behind her were diverted through a neighborhood side street. Kami told her teacher she was worried that one of those cars could be her mom's. Shortly thereafter, her teacher received a call from someone saying Kami had been in an accident. Since the teacher had just spoken with Kami and knew she was okay, that meant the car Kami had said was similar to her mom's was potentially one of the cars involved in the accident. With all the excitement, the caller most likely got the details mixed up.

In the past, I had two magnetic signs, one on each side of my car, advertising my real-estate business and phone number; however, several weeks before the accident, one of the signs was stolen. Left with only one sign, I thought it would look better on the back of the Expedition rather than on one side. Since the first car that stopped to assist at the accident scene parked behind my Expedition, the sign was not readily visible when Kami passed by, so she didn't know for sure whether it was my car. She called me, and when I did not answer, she knew in her heart that I was in one of those cars. This is the painful part: I would have taken crushed legs, a demolished ankle, broken ribs and a broken arm, and a collapsed lung over having my kids live through that nightmare. Most parents would feel just the same. But with God's help and the help of the many people He provided to surround us with love and prayers, we got through the ordeal together.

There must have been countless calls being made simultaneously. Someone had seen the sign on the back of my car and called my office. The only agent in the office that early was a gentleman with whom I attend church. He made the necessary calls and then called our church, which was how I was added to the prayer chains even while I was still trapped in the wreckage. I had worked at Compaq/HP for years. Many members of our congregation work there, so the prayer requests went out over the entire city quickly and were nationwide by that night. One of the ladies from church went to Walgreen's to be with Kami so that she wouldn't be alone. One of the assistant principals was sent to see if my son, Trey, was in school. Since my Expedition's final resting place was facing the school, there was speculation that the accident might have happened on the way to school and that Trey might still be in the car with me. Yet again, this was another prayer answered—Trey was already safe and sound at school. Classes had just begun, when Trey was asked to follow the assistant principal. He was happy to be excused from class but had no idea why. However, when they left the school grounds and crossed the street, heading toward Walgreen's, he knew something was wrong. Kami met Trey outside of Walgreen's, where they were told that I had been in a car accident. They stood there for a while, and then Kami began to panic. As part of her EMT training, she had learned that Life Flight never turned the rotors off if there was any possibility they would be transporting someone to a hospital. She could hear the blades continue to whirl—and then they stopped. Her heart seemed also to stop as panic overtook her. She did not know how many people were injured or how many ambulances had been there and left, but to her, the silence of the helicopter was an obvious indication that someone had not survived the crash.

A dear, sweet friend took both of my children to the chapel at our church to await word from Father Rob. He finally arrived and told them I had been flown to Hermann Hospital in Houston

Medical Center, but they didn't know any more than that. They spent the day with friends. I was able to speak with my daughter later that afternoon, just long enough to try to assure her that I would be fine. But she was not convinced.

So my rescue, at least here, is pretty obvious. How about yours? *Rescue* is an interesting term. We hear Jesus use words like *save, free, set free, liberate, release, let go, redeem,* and *abandon*. These are all words we are familiar with but don't necessarily associate with the word *rescue*.

Let's look at a different type of rescue. Sometimes we need to be rescued from worry or confusion. Early on, I recalled a dream I had while trapped in the car. It was clear yet confusing. I distinctly remember dreaming of someone speaking to me in what seemed to be an angry voice. Why was I dreaming about that while trapped, when all the while I was also feeling such comfort that so many were there to help me? I later came to realize what I mistook for anger was actually desperation.

The strangest part was that the voice in the dream was talking to me using the word *you* instead of *I* or *me*. It didn't make sense to me. The voice was not from anyone on the scene. Why would I be dreaming then anyway? Who would be angry with me, and how did the person know to say those things? I was hearing words of encouragement to bring me to a conscious awareness in order to assist my rescuers. These were not words anyone around me at that time would have known to say to me. One thing I learned firsthand through this experience is to be patient and listen.

This dream haunted me for about eight months. By that time, I had been walking for a few months. One day, I was out shopping with Kami and decided to try on some shoes. Shoe shopping, for me, was special, as I had thought I would never be able to wear shoes again, and here I was, trying on some darling plaid clogs! Although I couldn't walk well in them, just being able to try them on was awesome. My exuberance must have been obvious, since a woman nearby commented on the cute shoes. As we began to talk, she shared the joy of how good God can be in carrying us through in times of need. Just then, Kami rounded the corner, and I introduced her to my new friend. I wasn't surprised that Kami began to tell her about the accident, but it did surprise me that she began by talking about things that had occurred several months after the accident. I couldn't help but feel there was an underlying connection. Kami went on to say that one day in her EMT class, another trainer had been there to instruct them about the various extrication techniques. Kami had asked him if he was familiar with the accident on Louetta Road. He'd told her his team had been responsible for extricating the woman in the Expedition. She'd told him that woman was her mother. I had heard her tell this part before, but I'd always felt she was holding back some of the details from me. Kami continued to tell her that the rescue teams had arrived, assessed the situation, and determined how to get the car off my legs, but at that moment, I had woken and explained that my right ankle was trapped. I distinctly remembered this conversation for the first time! I had just pieced together that the dream I had in the car was, in fact, not a dream but a voice trying to wake me up. It all began to make sense. Someone had been trying diligently to wake me, but it was not working. At the last moment, I had awakened and had that conversation with the team about my ankle. Later, when I met David, the firefighter who had tried to release the ankle from the wreckage, he corroborated this story. If I had not awakened at that moment, they would have continued with the extrication plan, which would have also removed my ankle. Had these separate meetings and conversations not happened, it would not have been so clear that God had been the one who rescued me. I learned another life lesson: learn to pause and reflect on all that God has created. Listen to Him as well as to one another. Hidden blessings will then be revealed each day with everyone you meet.

This time, He rescued me from myself. In those early weeks, it became obvious to me and to those around me. I was becoming obsessed with knowing who the man in the window was. I had to know! I remembered that he appeared to be looking at me through a tunnel. Looking back, I suspect that as I awakened while lying on the driver's-side window, looking up, it was the man coming through the passenger's-side window. Everyone looked at me as if I were talking in a medicated fog. Later, I explained that he was big, meaning wide in the shoulders, like a firefighter. When I finally saw the police photos, I was amazed. In fact, there were photos of many firefighters looking in the passenger's-side window that day. Although I remembered that view of the firefighter in the passenger's window, it was the man in the front window whom I wanted to know. It's likely there was never a man in the front window, as I had pictured in my mind. Since the car was overturned and against the brick wall and the front end of the car was squashed, I am not sure how a man's face could have been in that space, but my vision remained, much to the chagrin of everyone else.

Several years later, I called the fire station. The chief invited me to attend one of their Monday weekly meetings, so I did. I had a burning desire to let these men know how much I appreciated all they had done that day, but I felt my words weren't enough. They were so gracious to me. Not only did they remember that day, but also, it had helped them develop some new training techniques since my accident had posed some new challenges.

I asked, "So who was the man in the window?" I will never forget the chief's response: "It was Boo Boo." I had to chuckle to myself. *Well isn't this fine? Yogi and Boo Boo came to rescue me! Leave it to me to have cartoon characters as my rescuers!* I was both amused and confused. But I listened. Boo Boo, it turned out, was a nickname for a local real-estate agent named David. I knew he was a successful agent, and eventually, I called him but had to leave a voice message. He didn't return my call, so months later, I called him again, and again he did not return my call. Eventually, I was able to reach him and spoke with him on the phone. He calmly said that he had known I would get in touch with him when the time was right. His words were comforting. We arranged to meet for lunch. I was nervous but anxious to thank him in person and explain that I would never be able to thank him enough—not only on my own behalf for saving my life but also for making it possible for my children to grow up with their mom. My gratefulness was deeper than my words could express.

As we ate, we talked. He told me he had never left my side. Does that sound familiar? God says He will never leave your side either, but we don't often remember this.

David explained that his job was to work on getting my ankle released. Up until I met him, I had not known this. He was cautious not to describe the goriness of the scene—he said only that they had worked diligently to free my right ankle. See how the pieces come together over time? God's plans for us work the same way. We must be patient and wait until God's perfect time.

As I heard him describe how he'd yelled to his partner to get the crowbar, I knew God had sent this angel to rescue me. I remembered hearing a calm voice next to me in the car. It had been David's comforting voice. Suddenly, I realized he had not seen my legs since that day, so with childlike exuberance, I offered to show him the ankle he had worked so hard to save. As he stood up, the color drained from his face, and he looked terrified. Then I realized what he must be thinking, so I told him to sit down so that I could fill him in on my life since that day.

Once I had been released from the hospital, I had a talk with my kids. I had seen how wearying this ordeal was on everyone who bore the burden of becoming my caretakers. I had told them we needed to laugh through this whole experience. As my legs had begun to heal, my kids had quickly told people that I was faking this whole thing—"Just look at that right leg!" How could both bones in the leg have been completely severed and the ankle bones crushed, yet they looked so normal now?

With a puzzled look on his face, David stood up once again. I raised my pant leg to expose my ankle. As he looked in amazement, tears ran down his face. He could finally see the fruit of his labor.

Not only did I have my ankle, but also, it looked as if nothing ever had happened to it.

I had intended to describe how I finally had been rescued from my obsession to meet the man in the window. He was my original focus, but what God unveiled that day was much more than the answer to my questions. I met the man whom God placed there to be an integral part of getting me out of the car, but as I listened to David, I began to realize a much deeper meaning. We sometimes need to search for answers, but we must also be prepared for some answers we didn't expect. By the simple act of reaching out to meet David, I found I became able to answer his questions as to what had ultimately happened to me. But even more, I learned that taking the time to thank those who have helped us in some way or influenced or impacted our hearts becomes a gift in itself. You never know how you will be rescued or whom you might rescue. Take time to tell others when and how they have touched you.

So I learned that the entire rescue was a team effort, with many people working together in the heat of the moment, against the clock, but it took me six months to piece this all together. I now know just how much divine presence there was that day!

> *The Lord saw how great man's wickedness on the earth had become, and that every inclination of the thoughts of his heart was only evil all the time. The Lord was grieved that he had made man on the earth, and his heart was filled with pain. So the Lord said, "I will wipe mankind, whom I have created, from the face of the earth—men and animals, and creatures that move along the ground, and birds of the air—for I am grieved that I have made them." But Noah found favor in the eyes of the Lord.*
>
> *"I am going to bring floodwaters on the earth to destroy all life under the heavens, every creature that has the breath of life in it. Everything on earth will perish. But I will establish*

my covenant with you, and you will enter the ark—you and your sons and your wife and your sons' wives with you. You are to bring into the ark two of all living creatures, male and female, to keep them alive with you."

For forty days the flood kept coming on the earth, and as the waters increased they lifted the ark high above the earth. The water rose and increased greatly on earth, and the ark floated on the surface of the water. They rose greatly on the earth, and all the high mountains under the entire heavens were covered. The waters rose and covered the mountains to a depth of more than twenty feet. Every living thing that moved on the earth perished—birds, livestock, wild animals, all the creatures that swarm over the earth, and all mankind. Everything on dry land that had the breath of life in its nostrils died. Every living thing on the face of the earth was wiped out: men and animals and the creatures that move along the ground and the birds of the air were wiped from the earth. Only Noah was left, and those with him in the ark. Genesis 6:5–8, 17–19; 7:17–23 (NIV)

During the fourth watch of the night Jesus went out to them, walking on the lake. When the disciples saw him walking on the lake, they were terrified. "It's a ghost," they said, and cried out in fear. But Jesus immediately said to them: "Take courage! It is I. Don't be afraid." "Lord, if it's you," Peter replied, "tell me to come to you on the water." "Come," he said. Then Peter got down out of the boat, walked on the water and came toward Jesus. But when he saw the wind, he was afraid and, beginning to sink, cried out, "Lord, save me!" Immediately Jesus reached out his hand and caught him. "You of little faith," he said, "why did you doubt?" And when they climbed into the boat, the wind died down.

> *Then those who were in the boat worshipped him, saying, "Truly you are the son of God."* Matthew 14:25–33 (NIV)

> *All who rely on observing the law are under a curse, for it is written: "Cursed is everyone who does not continue to do everything written in the Book of the Law." Clearly no one is justified before God by the law, because, "The righteous will live by faith." The law is not based on faith: on the contrary, "The man who does these things will live by them." Christ redeemed us from the curse of the law by becoming a curse for us, for it is written: "Cursed is everyone who is hung on a tree." He redeemed us in order that the blessing given to Abraham might come to the Gentiles through Christ Jesus, so that by faith we might receive the promise of the Spirit.* Galatians 3:10–14 (NIV)

The entire purpose of God sending His son to earth was to rescue us. The big picture of my rescue is easy to see. By looking at the smaller details, we see the many ways Jesus rescues us each and every day, just as He did the entire time He walked this earth in human form. It is my desire to share my experiences from March 28, 2006, onward. In so doing, I hope my words will inspire you to recognize God's many blessings in your own life and times He has rescued you that might have otherwise gone unnoticed.

> *Joshua said to all the people, "This is what the Lord, the God of Israel says: 'Long ago your forefathers, including Terah the father of Abraham and Nahor, lived beyond the River and worshiped other gods. But I took your father Abraham from the land beyond the River and led him throughout Canaan and gave him many descendants. I gave him Isaac, and to Isaac I gave Jacob and Esau. I assigned the hill country of Seir to Esau, but Jacob and his sons went down to Egypt.*

"'Then I sent Moses and Aaron, and I afflicted the Egyptians by what I did there, and I brought you out. When I brought your fathers out of Egypt, you came to the sea, and the Egyptians pursued them with chariots and horsemen as far as the Red Sea. But they cried to the Lord for help, and he put darkness between you and the Egyptians; he brought the sea over them and covered them. You saw with your own eyes what I did to the Egyptians. Then you lived in the desert for a long time.

"'I brought you to the land of the Amorites who lived east of the Jordan. They fought against you, but I gave them into your hands. I destroyed them from before you, and you took possession of their land. When Balak son of Zippor, the king of Moab, prepared to fight against Israel, he sent for Balaam son of Beor to put a curse on you. But I would not listen to Balaam so he blessed you again and again, and I delivered you out of his hand.

"'Then you crossed the Jordan and came to Jericho. The citizens of Jericho fought against you, as did also the Amorites, Perizzites, Canaanites, Hittitites, Girgashites, Hivites and Jebusites, but I gave them into your hands. I sent the hornet ahead of you, which drove them out before you—also the two Amorite kings. You did not do it with your own sword and bow. So I gave you a land on which you did not toil and cities you did not build; and you live in them and eat from vineyards and olive groves that you did not plant.'" Joshua 24:2–13 (NIV)

"Do not be afraid of them, for I am with you and will rescue you," declares the Lord. Jeremiah 1:8 (NIV)

"I will make you a wall to this people, a fortified wall of bronze; they will fight against you but will not overcome you, for I am with you to rescue and save you," declares the Lord. "I will save you from the hands of the wicked and redeem you from the grasp of the cruel." Jeremiah 15:20–21 (NIV)

Sometimes it takes a lifetime to see how the rescue takes place.

3

HELP ARRIVES WITH PRECISE TIMING

"Have no fear of sudden disaster or of the ruin that overtakes the wicked, for the Lord will be at your side and will keep your foot from being snared."
~Proverbs 3:25–26 (NIV)

It's amazing to see all that God has meticulously pieced together—if we take the time to notice. I think that is the key—we must take the time to notice. I believe His timing is and always has been precise. Only after close examination can we appreciate the intricate details that amaze us—only when we take the time.

I call this the doorbell story. Years ago, my husband and I purchased a home. We noticed that the doorbell lit up but didn't always ring when the button was pushed. We had it repaired several times, but the ringing still seemed to be inconsistent.

For the first few months after the accident, a nurse stayed with me during the day, since I needed assistance for everything. One day—I believe it was the day of my first doctor's appointment after returning home from the hospital—I was uneasy about having to rely on my nurse to accompany me. This was a completely new way of life for me, having to depend completely on help from others. People from my church and many others offered to help. Although I was told there were many ways in which I should allow people to help me, it was hard to accept that I needed help. To those who knew me, my accepting help was, in itself, a miracle. Like many of you, I am reluctant to ask for help so as not to inconvenience anyone.

I had to get over that. I called on the Ground Angels, a group from my church, for assistance. They were volunteers who would drive me to appointments. One dear friend, Bob, became my driver. At first, I was comfortable with Bob driving me but then the "mom" feelings kicked in, and it bothered me to have Bob watch as I struggled to do anything. I could be loaded into a vehicle in only one direction, since I had only one arm to assist in the undertaking. Then the wheelchair had to be loaded into the trunk. I hated seeing this gentleman, who is a senior citizen, have to do the heavy lifting for me and of me.

I had been coached, in no uncertain terms, to be sure I took my pain meds. You might think that taking my pain medicine would be logical, knowing what I had just been through, but to know me is to know I hate taking meds. I did, however, heed their advice because there were others who had to take care of me, and I didn't want to make it any harder on them. To prepare for this first doctor's visit, I took my pain meds, calculating that I should fall asleep on the ride home.

Guess what? It didn't happen that way at all! The doctors were running late. Once I got into an examining room, I began to feel the effects of the meds. The doctors finally came in to fit me for my boots. They were in and out of the room, attending to all the details. But hard as I tried to remain alert, I began to feel as if I were going to faint from exhaustion. It's terribly hard to faint in a wheelchair. I finally admitted to anyone who would listen that I desperately needed help—now! The doctors and nurses didn't know how to help either. Somehow, they got me over to the examining table and tried to lay my head down. Lying down helped for a moment. I regained a little strength as they put on the enormous boots, and Bob and my nurse began the ordeal of getting me in and out of the car and back home to bed.

I slept for hours after the eventful outing. About dinnertime, my husband walked into the bedroom, having let the nurse leave for the day. He was lighthearted, but I was on another plane of thought altogether.

As he greeted me, I began to rant. "I am done," I told him. "I have been good for all these weeks. I have not complained. I have done exactly what the doctors have asked. I am just plain done. Take the boots off. I Am Done! I'm walking out of here. I have done all that was asked of me, and I'm walking out!" It was not the physical pain that was getting to me; it was that I felt as if I were an observer of my situation, almost as if I weren't there. Having been such an active, strong woman, now enduring complete dependence on others simply for my daily needs made me feel I was a burden to everyone around me. That feeling was more than I could handle. I was done!

Matt's eyes were as wide as saucers. He had no idea how to respond to my tirade. His normally calm and submissive wife had lost it. Of course, just as I announced that I was done and he needed to take the boots off so that I could walk out of the room, the doorbell rang—the same inconsistent doorbell of old. He didn't know whether to answer the door or try to reason with me. He answered the door and then ran back to me. I asked who it was, but in his haste, he didn't get the name right. He shuffled back and forth, in and out of the bedroom, to and from the front door. Finally, I told him to invite the visitor into the bedroom, where I was.

It was a woman I knew from our neighborhood. Our sons had played on several sports teams together over the years. She had brought dinner. She was calm and not appalled by my physical condition, and she certainly was not aware of the emotional outburst my husband had just witnessed.

As we began to chat, discussing the specifics of the accident and recovery process, she revealed her own story. As a teen, she too had been in a nasty car accident. She'd suffered a severe leg injury that had required quite a bit of physical therapy. We discussed scars and how women perceive the enormity of what they can do to us. I listened as this woman walked into my home after using my sometimes-broken doorbell, which happened to actually ring on that night. She came to tell me her story, which was exactly what I would soon experience. She spoke of how she had to surrender in order to allow others to help her. She had persevered to recover, all the while placing her complete faith in God. She had recovered—at least, it appeared to me that she had—both physically and emotionally and had gone on to live a normal life. Then she left. I was floored! God had sent someone right to my bedside at that precise moment and with the exact lesson I needed to hear!

These are the things that make me so passionate to share God's love with all. It's fun to see His work as it is happening. It's a matter of learning to be intentional about opening your eyes and heart to life around you. Soak in the sights and sounds and allow God to show you how He *"causes all things to work together for good"* Romans 8:28 (NASB) when we surrender our will to His.

God is continually demonstrating His love and mercy. We just need to pay attention in order to appreciate all that He puts out there so that we can learn of His love and know that He is always there to help.

Here's another story—one that is completely different but demonstrates the same lesson. My husband had unloaded me from the car at church. We propped my legs up on the bench outside while he parked the car. While I was waiting, a friend walked up and began to speak to me. At first, her conversation struck me as being a little odd. She asked how long I would be in the wheelchair. I wasn't offended. In fact, by this time, I was accustomed to seeing the shocked expressions and the reluctance of people to approach me in the chair. This interaction was different.

I had just been to the orthopedic surgeon on Friday. My home physical therapist had been hoping the surgeon would allow me to put some weight on both legs and try walking. I knew in my heart that wasn't going to happen at that appointment, but I allowed myself to hope that he might suggest it. He did not. He wasn't happy that I even asked him when he thought I could walk. He bent over to look at me eye-to-eye only to say plainly, "You have legs!" I knew exactly what he meant, and indeed, I was thankful I hadn't lost them completely. While the surgeons initially put my legs back together, they weren't convinced that I would be able to keep them. My body seemed to begin the healing process, but *begin* is the operative word here. My surgeon could see some evidence in one of my legs that the bones were beginning to repair. I instantly chimed in an attempt to break the tension that now filled the room. That evening, while sitting outside, it finally sunk in. I was beginning to realize that I could be sitting in this wheelchair for another year—my interpretation! I asked my husband to sit down. I explained to him that the bones were beginning to show some potential healing but that there was a long way to go. We needed to be prepared for the possibility that I might be sitting in this chair for a long time. It was a private and somber weekend.

Now someone had specifically asked me how long I would be in a wheelchair. Most people didn't understand that, from a medical perspective, I would likely never walk. I didn't accept that prognosis. I knew I would walk again. I did not know when, or even if it would be with my own legs, but I did know I would somehow walk again.

This friend asked me if aquatics was being included as part of my physical therapy. I told her that it was not and hadn't even been mentioned as far as I was knew. I updated her on the specifics of my current therapy regime. She said that she was a physical therapist in aquatics. Since my prognosis was now an extensive stay in the wheelchair, she suggested I call my doctor for his opinion. I did, and he thought doing aquatics was a fabulous idea. Since her facility was not close, she offered to pick me up on her way to work several days a week, and other people offered to take me home.

Aquatic physical therapy was by far the best thing I could have done. I was surprised to see that I no longer thought I had legs to move. The process of getting into the facility, changing clothes, and getting to the pool and the apparatus to lower me into the pool was exhausting. Of course, I had on a life jacket. The instructors gave me a noodle to sit on and told me to kick to the other end of the pool. I was shocked. It was like asking me to speak Russian. I had no idea where to begin. The concept of moving my legs was completely foreign to me. It took tremendous concentration to move my lower legs. The slightest pressure of the water on my shins produced almost unbearable pain. I worked with them for several months. Not only was this exercise good for muscle development in my legs, arms, and torso, but also, my brain was retrained to communicate with my legs to produce movement. Who would have thought that would be the biggest challenge? And it was amazing to realize that God had placed this dear lady there on that Sunday, at that bench, with the suggestion of aquatic physical therapy and had even provided a carpool to get me there!

Here's the clincher: right after I completed my rehab at the aquatic center, my friend moved to another state. As I look back, it becomes clear that God had a plan all along. We don't often reflect on how much God is present in the details of our lives.

Trust Him! He'll be with you or send someone to help you in your time of need, just as He did for me!

> *Then the LORD said to Moses, "Tell the Israelites to turn back and encamp near Pi Hahiroth, between Migdol and the sea. They are to encamp by the sea, directly opposite Baal Zephon. Pharaoh will think, 'The Israelites are wandering around the land in confusion, hemmed in by the desert.' And I will harden Pharaoh's heart, and he will pursue them. But I will gain glory for myself through Pharaoh and all his army, and the Egyptians will know that I am the LORD.'" So the Israelites did this.*

> *When the king of Egypt was told that the people had fled, Pharaoh and his officials changed their minds about them and said, "What have we done? We have let the Israelites go and have lost their services!" So he had his chariot made ready and took his army with him. He took six hundred of the best chariots, along with all the other chariots of Egypt, with officers over all of them. The LORD hardened the heart of Pharaoh king of Egypt, so that he pursued the Israelites, who were marching out boldly. The Egyptians— all Pharaoh's horses and chariots, horsemen and troops— pursued the Israelites and overtook them as they camped by the sea near Pi Hahiroth, opposite Baal Zephon.*

> *As Pharaoh approached, the Israelites looked up, and there were the Egyptians, marching after them. They were terrified and cried out to the LORD. They said to Moses, "Was it because there were no graves in Egypt that you brought us to the desert to die? What have you done to us by bringing us out of Egypt? Didn't we say to you in Egypt, 'Leave us alone;*

let us serve the Egyptians'? It would have been better for us to serve the Egyptians than to die in the desert!"

Moses answered the people, "Do not be afraid. Stand firm and you will see the deliverance the LORD will bring to you today. The Egyptians you see today you will never see again. The LORD will fight for you; you need only to be still."

Then the LORD said to Moses, "Why are you crying out to me? Tell the Israelites to move on. Raise your staff and stretch out your hand over the sea to divide the water so that the Israelites can go through the sea on dry ground. I will harden the hearts of the Egyptians so that they will go in after them. And I will gain glory through Pharaoh and all his army, through his chariots and his horsemen. The Egyptians will know that I am the LORD when I gain glory through Pharaoh, his chariots and his horsemen."

Then the angel of God, who had been traveling in front of Israel's army, withdrew and went behind them. The pillar of cloud also moved from in front and stood behind them, coming between the armies of Egypt and Israel. Throughout the night the cloud brought darkness to the one side and light to the other side; so neither went near the other all night long.

Then Moses stretched out his hand over the sea, and all that night the LORD drove the sea back with a strong east wind and turned it into dry land. The waters were divided, and the Israelites went through the sea on dry ground, with a wall of water on their right and on their left.

The Egyptians pursued them, and all Pharaoh's horses and chariots and horsemen followed them into the sea. During the last watch of the night the LORD looked down from the *pillar of the fire and cloud at the Egyptian army and threw it into confusion. He made the wheels of their chariots come off so that they had difficulty driving. And the Egyptians said, "Let's get away from the Israelites! The LORD is fighting for them against Egypt."*

Then the LORD said to Moses, "Stretch out your hand over the sea so that the waters may flow back over the Egyptians and their chariots and horsemen." Moses stretched out his hand over the sea, and at daybreak the sea went back to its place. The Egyptians were fleeing toward it, and the LORD swept them into the sea. The water flowed back and covered the chariots and horsemen—the entire army of Pharaoh that had followed the Israelites into the sea. Not one of them survived. Exodus 14:1–31 (NIV)

After arresting him, he put him in prison, handing him over to be guarded by four squads of four soldiers each. Herod intended to bring him out for public trial after the Passover.

So Peter was kept in prison, but the church was earnestly praying to God for him.

The night before Herod was to bring him to trial, Peter was sleeping between two soldiers, bound with two chains, and sentries stood guard at the entrance. Suddenly an angel of the Lord appeared and a light shone in the cell. He struck Peter on the side and woke him up. "Quick, get up!" he said, and the chains fell off Peter's wrists.

Then the angel said to him, "Put on your clothes and sandals." And Peter did so. "Wrap your cloak around you and follow me," the angel told him. Peter followed him out of the prison, but he had no idea that what the angel was doing was really happening; he thought he was seeing a vision. They passed the first and second guards and came to the iron gate leading to the city. It opened for them by itself, and they went through it. When they had walked the length of one street, suddenly the angel left him.

Then Peter came to himself and said, "Now I know without a doubt that the Lord sent his angel and rescued me from Herod's clutches and from everything the Jewish people were anticipating." Acts 12:4–11 (NIV)

On the third day a wedding took place at Cana in Galilee. Jesus' mother was there, and Jesus and his disciples had also been invited to the wedding. When the wine was gone, Jesus' mother said to him, "They have no more wine."

"Dear woman why do you involve me?" Jesus replied. "My time has not yet Come."His mother said to the servants, "Do whatever he tells you."

Nearby stood six stone water jars, the kind used by the Jews for ceremonial washing, each holding from twenty to thirty gallons. Jesus said to the servants, "Fill the jars with water"; so they filled them to the brim.

Then he told them, "Now draw some out and take it to the master of the banquet." They did so, and the master of the banquet tasted the water that had been turned into wine. He did not realize where it had come from, though the servants who had drawn the water knew. Then he called the bridegroom aside and said, "Everyone brings out the choice wine after the guests have had too much to drink; but you have saved the best till now."

> *This, the first of his miraculous signs, Jesus performed at Cana in Galilee. He thus revealed his glory, and his disciples put their faith in him.* John 2:11 (NIV)

In this instance, we are told the entire story, so we are privileged to see the miracle of Jesus turning water into wine for the wedding guests. He was there to help. This was the beginning of his public display of miracles recorded in God's Word so that we may read with our minds and learn in our hearts who He is and why He came. But this is also a remarkable story in another light, when we take a closer look. What about all those guests at the wedding, tasting the wine? They were part of Jesus' first miracle here on Earth, and they had no idea. How often do we receive God's gifts or become part of God's plan to deliver His gifts to others and never even know it? Might we be missing out on some of God's blessings?

> *Now Daniel so distinguished himself among the administrators and the satraps by his exceptional qualities that the king planned to set him over the whole kingdom. At this, the administrators and satraps tried to find grounds for charges against Daniel in his conduct of government affairs, but they were unable to do so. They could find no corruption in him, because he was trustworthy and neither corrupt nor negligent. Finally these men said, "We will never find any basis for charges against this man Daniel unless it has something to do with the law of his God."*

> *So the administrators and the satraps went as a group to the king and said: "O King Darius, live forever! The royal administrators, prefects, satraps, advisers and governors have all agreed that the king should issue an edict and enforce the decree that anyone who prays to any god or man during the next thirty days, except to you, O king, shall be thrown into the lions' den. Now, O king, issue the decree and put it in*

writing so that it cannot be altered—in accordance with the laws of the Medes and Persians, which cannot be repealed." So King Darius put the decree in writing.

Now when Daniel learned that the decree had been published, he went home to his upstairs room where the windows opened toward Jerusalem. Three times a day he got down on his knees and prayed, giving thanks to his God, just as he had done before. Then these men went as a group and found Daniel praying and asking God for help. So they went to the king and spoke to him about his royal decree: "Did you not publish a decree that during the next thirty days anyone who prays to any god or man except to you, O king, would be thrown into the lions' den?"

The king answered, "The decree stands--in accordance with the laws of the Medes and Persians, which cannot be repealed."

Then they said to the king, "Daniel, who is one of the exiles from Judah, pays no attention to you, O king, or to the decree you put in writing. He still prays three times a day." When the king heard this, he was greatly distressed; he was determined to rescue Daniel and made every effort until sundown to save him.

Then the men went as a group to the king and said to him, "Remember, O king, that according to the law of the Medes and Persians no decree or edict that the king issues can be changed."

So the king gave the order, and they brought Daniel and threw him into the lions' den. The king said to Daniel, "May your God, whom you serve continually, rescue you!"

A stone was brought and placed over the mouth of the den, and the king sealed it with his own signet ring and with the rings of his nobles, so that Daniel's situation might not be changed. Then the king returned to his palace and spent the night without eating and without any entertainment being brought to him. And he could not sleep.

At the first light of dawn, the king got up and hurried to the lions' den. When he came near the den, he called to Daniel in an anguished voice, "Daniel, servant of the living God, has your God whom you serve continually, been able to rescue you from the lions?"

Daniel answered, "O king, live forever! My God sent his angel, and he shut the mouths of the lions. They have not hurt me, because I was found innocent in his sight. Nor have I ever done any wrong before you, O king."

The king was overjoyed and gave orders to lift Daniel out of the den. And when Daniel was lifted from the den, no wound was found on him, because he had trusted in his God.

At the king's command, the men who had falsely accused Daniel were brought in and thrown into the lions' den, along with their wives and children. And before they reached the floor of the den, the lions overpowered them and crushed all their bones. Daniel 6:3–24 (NIV)

Then he got into the boat and his disciples followed him. Without warning, a furious storm came up on the lake, so that the waves swept over the boat. But Jesus was sleeping. The disciples went and woke him, saying, "Lord, save us! We're going to drown!"

> *He replied, "You of little faith, why are you so afraid?" Then he got up and rebuked the winds and the waves and it was completely calm.*
>
> *The men were amazed and asked, "What kind of man is this? Even the winds and the waves obey him!"*
> Matthew 8:23–27 (NIV)

Here is yet another straightforward story of a specific time and place when Jesus was there to help. Maybe there wasn't a physical need for help, but nonetheless, they were in fear, and someone called to Him—and He was there.

How often do we cry for help, possibly unnecessarily? If we keep our hearts and eyes open to look at the whole situation, we can usually see that God has either sent someone to help us in some way or revealed the way, through His Word, in which we must go. In hindsight, we can sometimes learn from having endured the hardship. He really does have precise timing. His timing is perfect! We just need to be still and know that He is God.

> *The whole Israelite community set out from the Desert of Sin, traveling from place to place as the LORD commanded. They camped at Rephidim, but there was no water for the people to drink. So they quarreled with Moses and said, "Give us water to drink."*
>
> *Moses replied, "Why do you quarrel with me? Why do you put the LORD to the test?"*
>
> *But the people were thirsty for water there, and they grumbled against Moses. They said, "Why did you bring us up out of Egypt to make us and our children and livestock die of thirst?"*

Then Moses cried out to the LORD, "What am I to do with these people? They are almost ready to stone me."

The LORD answered Moses, "Walk on ahead of the people. Take with you some of the elders of Israel and take in your hand the staff with which you struck the Nile, and go. I will stand there before you by the rock at Horeb. Strike the rock, and water will come out of it for the people to drink." So Moses did this in the sight of the elders of Israel. And he called the place Massah and Meribah because the Israelites quarreled and because they tested the LORD saying, "Is the LORD among us or not?" Exodus 17:1–7 (NIV)

The LORD said to Moses, "I have heard the grumbling of the Israelites. Tell them, 'At twilight you will eat meat, and in the morning you will be filled with bread. Then you will know that I am the LORD your God.'"

That evening quail came and covered the camp, and in the morning there was a layer of dew around the camp. When the dew was gone, thin flakes like frost on the ground appeared on the desert floor. When the Israelites saw it, they said to each other, "What is it?" For they did not know what it was.

Moses said to them, "It is the bread the LORD has given you to eat. This is what the LORD has commanded: 'Each one is to gather as much as he needs. Take an omer for each person you have in your tent.'"

Each morning, everyone gathered as much as he needed, and when the sun grew hot, it melted away. Exodus 16:11–16, 21 (NIV)

Some time later God tested Abraham. He said to him, "Abraham!" "Here I am," he replied.

Then God said, "Take your son, your only son, Isaac, whom you love, and go to the region of Moriah. Sacrifice him there as a burnt offering on one of the mountains I will tell you about."

Early the next morning Abraham got up and saddled his donkey. He took with him two of his servants and his son Isaac. When he had cut enough wood for the burnt offering, he set out for the place God had told him about. On the third day Abraham looked up and saw the place in the distance. He said to his servants, "Stay here with the donkey while I and the boy go over then. We will worship and then we will come back to you."

Abraham took the wood for the burnt offering and placed it on his son Isaac, and he himself carried the fire and the knife. As the two of them went on together, Isaac spoke up and said to his father Abraham, "Father?"

"Yes, my son?" Abraham replied. "The fire and the wood are here," Isaac said, "but where is the lamb for the burnt offering?"

Abraham answered, "God himself will provide the lamb for the burnt offering, my son." And the two of them went on together.

When they reached the place God had told him about, Abraham built an altar there and arranged the wood on it. He bound his son Isaac and laid him on the altar, on top of the wood. Then he reached out his hand and took the knife to slay his son. But the angel of the LORD called out to him from heaven, "Abraham! Abraham!"

"Here I am," he replied. "Do not lay a hand on the boy," he said. "Do not do anything to him. Now I know that you fear God, because you have not withheld from me your son, your only son."

Abraham looked up and there in a thicket he saw a ram caught by its horns. He went over and took the ram and sacrificed it as a burnt offering instead of his son. So Abraham called that place the LORD Will Provide. And to this day it is said, "On the mountain of the LORD it will be provided."

The angel of the LORD called to Abraham from heaven a second time and said, "I swear by myself, declares the LORD, that because you have done this and have not withheld your son, your only son, I will surely bless you and make your descendants as numerous as the stars in the sky and as the sand on the seashore. Your descendants will take possession of the cities of their enemies, and through your offspring all nations on earth will be blessed, because you have obeyed me." Genesis 22:1–18 (NIV)

"Ask and it will be given to you; seek and you will find; knock and the door will be opened to you. For everyone who asks receives; he who seeks finds; and to him who knocks, the door will be opened." Matthew 7:7–8 (NIV)

It can't get much simpler than this. Ask the Lord for help. This idea is repeated in Luke 11:9–10 (NIV) *"So I say to you: Ask and it will be given to you; seek and you will find; knock and the door will be opened to you. For everyone who asks receives; he who seeks finds; and to him who knocks, the door will be opened."*

4

YOU NEVER KNOW WHEN

"Some people have entertained angels without knowing it."
~Hebrews 13:2b (NIV)

I learned a lesson following my accident that I would like to share with you. It is a lesson that has impacted my life so much that I now put it to use every day. You never know when you might influence someone. I am blessed to have friends and family who tell me when something I have said or done remains with them and inspires them in some way. This is a twofold blessing for me. To know that I influenced someone is beyond my comprehension. I am just living and telling the stories that undeniably show that God is with us every moment. If by sharing my experiences, someone finds help or comfort in some small way, I am overjoyed. But when they tell me what they have learned and as a result, this is even more exciting—so much so that I have decided to make a particular point of giving back to others who have helped me without knowing it. I feel I owe that gift to them—and what a gift it is!

I had a friend who called to check on me while I was still in the hospital. She told me that she couldn't deal with hospitals. Frankly, she wasn't the only one who expressed those feelings. She said she would visit me as soon as I got home. The accident happened on March 28, Easter was on April 16, and I was coming home for Easter. No one believed me. In fact, they all thought I must have had one too many doses of morphine. I knew I had to be at our Easter service. Both of my children were acolytes and would be serving that day. Another young man who had played a heartwarming role in the communications at the accident scene would also be serving as an acolyte that Sunday. It was unsettling to the hospital staff as well as to those who came to visit me in the hospital to hear me proclaim my intent to be at the church service that Easter Sunday, when the reality was that it was highly unlikely I would be able to do that. The priest from my church pulled my children aside and explained that their mom would not likely be home for Easter, in an attempt to prepare them so that they might not be as disappointed.

My son's sixteenth birthday was April 13. I was crushed that I was still in the hospital, but a friend brought a birthday cake decorated in a golf theme, and we celebrated in the hospital room.

It was amazing! Something this friend felt was such a small gesture meant the world to me and my children. Thank you, Bilinda! She was there not only for my son's birthday celebration but also every day for me and my kids. She would pray with me. She wrote a short prayer that I still keep with me. Her son drew a picture that I keep as well. These were seemingly small gestures, but they have meant so much to me all these years. They are precious memories.

The standard hospital procedure was to do new bloodwork to confirm everything was acceptable for patient release. Mine was not. The hospital staff went to extra lengths to retest until I was, in fact, released on Friday, April 14. This meant I could be at church on Easter with all the people who had prayed diligently, beginning while I was trapped in the car and continuing during my hospital stay. I wanted to be there for them and with them. I had no idea the impact my presence would make on them or me, and it's something I'll never forget.

That Easter Sunday morning was a reality check for me. I had nothing to offer but a smile. My daughter bought me a new outfit, one I could actually get into with a lot of help. As much as my heart was in this endeavor, I ended up fainting as my husband helped me dress. My family knew that all I wanted was to be at church on Easter Sunday; however, even I was beginning to doubt that I had the strength to go. But I was determined. We all knew I had to go. I didn't even know why I was so obsessed with this goal other than to show my gratitude for all the prayers and to show them I had survived and was there in answer to their prayers.

Of course, we were late. Sitting in the wheelchair, legs propped up, the gorgeous handmade quilt covering most of my damaged legs, I saw my friend Debbie. I had completely forgotten she was going to meet me there. I saw a look on her face that I would later recognize as shock and devastation at seeing me in a wheelchair and not knowing whether my situation would ever change. She stayed by my side as others awkwardly came up to greet me. They didn't know whether or not they should hug me, and they did not want to bump into my legs. Debbie was so sweet and protective of me all the while.

About ten months later, she approached me and began to talk with me in a serious tone. She asked if I remembered being in the back of the church on Easter Sunday, near her. I told her I did, and she went on to say that on that Easter morning, she'd had serious intentions of ending her life. While observing me, Debbie ultimately decided that if I could endure such adversity, so could she. I have no doubt that God put into my heart the determination to be at church on that Easter Sunday in order to accomplish His purpose for her life. I feel honored that God used me as an inspiration for her without my realizing it. We never know when God might use us to influence someone else.

I was telling my friend Dennis about a fabulous retreat I had attended about three and a half years after the accident. It was a spirit-filled weekend I shall never forget. It is a retreat I now often encourage others to experience. Several days later, Dennis called to say, "I was talking about you." Apparently, he had told a coworker about the weekend retreat experience and about me and the changes that had resulted since my accident. She had asked if I would be willing to share my experiences with her Bible study group at the office. I was thrilled to be offered the opportunity to tell what God has done for me. It amazes me when I realize that God miraculously intervenes to allow things to come together for His greater purpose.

I was nervous and unsure what I would say, but God was right there with me. He placed the right words in my heart to open a dialogue with this group, which led to a tearful time of sharing. We see every day how God's presence is in every aspect of our lives. My delight is in living for God, and I truly wish that same joy for others as well.

Several weeks later, I received a call from Dennis, who said, "A wise woman once told me if you pay attention and are patient, you may see how God pieces things together." He went on to explain that he had been in an awkward situation and had prayed that God would resolve it somehow. He had been frustrated for years. Then a frightening incident had occurred that had caused him to realize that if things had been different during all those years, the ending might have been tragic. Now he is able to see God's bigger plan. Sometimes when you don't like what you see, if you resolve to wait patiently, you might receive the joy of getting to watch God's plan unfold!

Not only had something I said resonated with this friend, but also, he had come back to share that news with me. What a blessing for us all! God's blessings never cease. When we share with one another and pass His blessings forward, they become known to many.

This same spirit-filled weekend retreat brought forth one of the most powerful signs that God is in control. Let me set the scene to give you some background. The retreat was geared toward high-school-aged youth. If there are enough adults in attendance at such retreats, they are welcomed to participate, although somewhat separately. Friday night was a meet-and-greet night.

Each participant selected a partner—someone he or she didn't already know—and asked questions of the partner in order to learn more about the other. I began talking to the lady next to me. Her name was Janice, and she had recently moved to New England. She had come back with her daughter to attend this retreat. We laughed as we asked each other silly questions, such as, "What color is your toothbrush?" or "What grade are you in?" After a time, one of the adult leaders instructed us to choose a different partner, since he assumed we had known each other previously. Janice and I argued with him, trying to convince him that we had only just met! We were both bothered by this interruption and his insistence that we "break it up." But the weekend was such an awesome experience that we soon forgot all about our introduction.

The next day, during a small adult group meeting, the friend who had driven me to the retreat asked if I would share with the group some of my experiences since the accident. I was happy to do so, and I closed my remarks with "It never ends." I continue to meet people who share their stories with me, and they frequently cause me to realize how things work together smoothly in God's plan. How exciting it is to see this continue to happen! Our small group was told to wrap it up, as we were being called to meet in a larger group session. As we were leaving, Janice asked to speak with me. She seemed upset and was anxious to talk. I told the group we would join them soon, but I needed to hear what Janice had to say. At first, I thought she might have had bad news from home, temporarily forgetting she had been right there with me the whole time, and we didn't have cell phones.

She had a frightened look on her face. She began to tell me a story about her mother, who had undergone some surgery in the past. Janice had arranged to be with her for however long her recovery took. Unexpectedly, her mom came down with an infection that required both of her ankles to be amputated. The infection progressed, and Janice painfully watched as the surgeons had to remove more and more of her mom's legs over almost a year's time. Janice kept her vow to be with her mom in good days and bad. She was never sure if her mom's conversations were drug-induced or not, but she was there for her mother.

One day, Janice's mother asked her to come sit by her because she had something she wanted to tell her. Janice listened intently, though her mother's comments were confusing to her at the time. Her mom said that Janice would someday meet someone who would have "her legs." *What a strange thing to say,* Janice thought, but the memory of this unexplained message remained in the back of her mind for about three years before we met. My accident was March 28; her mother's birthday is March 28. Unbeknownst to Janice, ever since the accident, I have said that my legs are not *my* legs. So this was an even more powerful message to me. My family knows that my own mom sent me a photo of herself, my daughter, and me, taken just months before the accident. My reaction upon seeing it was "That was when I had legs." I do, in fact, have my own legs; they are slightly bionic, but they are mine. However, they have never felt as if they were mine. Most people don't understand this. So when

Janice revealed to me what her mom had said to her, we were both awestruck. That night, I asked the leader if I could take a moment to share something with the group. I explained to them why I had left my discussion group earlier and told them of my conversation with Janice. God's revelations never end, and I get to share with others and they with me. Then I asked Janice to tell them what she had told me as we walked out earlier. As you can imagine, there was complete silence. At the end of the miraculous weekend, Janice gave me the bracelet that she, her daughters, and her mother had all worn. It is a James Avery bracelet—*"And Lo, I am with you always"*. Matthew 28:20b (NASB) Isn't God awesome? And of course, my story with Janice and her family doesn't end there.

I recently read an article about a doctor who became paralyzed and immediately began to apologize to his wife because he knew life would forever be changed for them. Since life would be different, he assumed it would be a life of struggles. He went on to explain that what made life worth living was touch. (Others don't necessarily know what patients can feel, much less what feels normal.) God teaches us it's the little things that bring us delight. So once again, you never know in what way you might touch someone and potentially affect his or her life forever. As Hebrews 13:1–2 (NIV) says, *"Keep on loving each other as brothers. Do not forget to entertain strangers, for by so doing some people have entertained angels without knowing it."*

Maybe you need to reread that passage. God says you don't know whom you are talking to. Do you sometimes feel as if someone you talk to could be an angel that God has sent to you for that moment in time? It's like help arriving with precise timing—again! (See chapter 3.)

As I am sure you can imagine, the scar from the leg reconstruction was ugly at best. Although I was immeasurably thankful for both my legs, the reality was that I didn't think people needed to see them. One of my friends called to offer support and words of encouragement. He went on to say what a great testimony this whole accident had been—a real testament to what prayer and faith in God can do when we keep our focus on Him and place everything in His hands. He was right, but I was taken back and immediately thought of my leg looking awful and what a sight it would be should a mom come into my office with a child. The poor little thing would probably be traumatized! I shared the thought of this scene with my friend and my nurse. They didn't understand. Then I came to the realization that I was not living in praise to God for what He had done for me. I had thought I was, but I also realized this scene was a reality, and I needed to consider others too.

A few days later, my nurse told me she had been giving some thought to what I had said about my fears of other people, children in particular, seeing this mess of a leg. She said that as a woman, she agreed that people would notice the obvious injury and be appalled. She understood that although I lived in utter gratitude that I had both my legs, my legs were an ugly sight. As we were discussing this, my daughter walked in. She was a senior in high school and was going to graduate shortly. She had always planned to go into the medical field, so she saw much of my injury from a scientific standpoint.

As she joined in the conversation, she began to laugh. I was shocked at her reaction. Then she said, "Of course it's ugly! You can have plastic surgery later if you want to make it look better." That was exactly what I needed to hear. I had the acknowledgment that my left leg was terribly unattractive, with skin and muscle grafts covering the majority of the lower leg, However, I could now put that anxiety behind me and regain the joy that I was here, was healing, and was with my family, praising God for bringing us through this together. And no matter who might see my leg, it would be okay. As the scar healed, and with the event of another surgery on that leg, the scar greatly diminished on its own, so it is a great testimony that I will gladly share!

Several years after the accident, my attorney called me. He sounded a little anxious. He said he was posting a blog in which I would be the subject, so he was calling to get my permission. I was more than a little confused. What on earth would he be saying about me in a blog? I had not spoken with him in a while. He had been an attorney for twenty-five years or so and had obviously seen families go through a nightmare or two over the years. But for some reason, my story seemed to resonate with him. He said that he realized how many people are affected by a tragic accident like this. The injured people and their immediate families are not the only ones affected. So too are the churches, work places, and communities that have heard and seen the devastation. I would never have guessed in a million years that my life would have made him stop and think about the wide-reaching arms of destruction, but somehow it did.

So you never know whom or how many people you might touch through something you say or do or how you handle your troubles. Rest assured, however, that people are touched! Sharing experiences might be the perfect opportunity to walk through tough times together, with God's guidance and strength. Live in faith, and share the experience that others have gone through so that they too may feel God's love and pass His words on to others.

Here's another story of an unexpected tugging of the heartstrings. On one occasion, there were four teens in our house—three boys and a girl. As you can imagine, one boy can push the envelope in those wonder years, but with the crowd of three, you never know what might be coming your way. Tattoos and piercings were the topic at the time. As a parent, I felt that they were too young to make decisions that were permanent, and I took the stand that my kids should not be allowed to get a tattoo or piercing until they were at least eighteen years old. Personally, I don't think most are ready at eighteen to make any permanent decisions, but I did recognize that they were legally considered adults. Tattoos became nearly a daily discussion in my house. Nonetheless, my children seemed to realize that I set my rule with their best interests in mind.

Remember that my son, Trey, turned sixteen while I was in the hospital. At seventeen and a half, he came running down the stairs one afternoon, shouting that he was getting a tattoo—but he was waiting until he was eighteen! My mind was reeling. How was I going to handle the issue this time? What was I going to say? As I cautiously walked up the stairs, I saw that he was watching a program called *Ink*, about tattooing. Next to the TV was a desk with a computer on it. I watched as he continued to flip between two websites featuring tattoos. Then the words came out of his mouth: "I can't decide"—and that was all I heard! I thought, *Thank you, God, for interjecting this point at this moment.* Since I now had him where I wanted him, I began to settle down a bit. As I sat next to Trey, I saw what was on the screen—crosses of all kinds. He continued flipping back and forth between the two websites showing tattoos of crosses. He said he couldn't decide which cross to get. My mind and heart stopped! He continued, "I want to get a cross on the muscle of my arm with your name, for your strength." Wow! I could not believe my ears. My heart was overwhelmed. Trey had seen past the destruction of his mother physically and all that went with that. Our lives had changed completely, but he saw the power of prayer and faith. He saw family, neighbors, church members, and many people come together to support us all. He saw God's strength carrying us through. Of course, I was speechless.

At some point, what seemed like hours later, I could muster a few words, through the tears, to let him know how deeply touched I was that he wanted to honor me in that way. It now became clear why he had been asking what my given name was because he knew I retained my maiden name as my middle name once married--a seemingly confusing tradition to a young boy. All along, he was secretly planning the tattoo as his story—his testimony of what God revealed to him through it all.

Eventually, I did turn back into the mom, reiterating the fact that his indecisiveness meant he should wait a little longer. He is now twenty-two and has graduated from college. He talks about the design of the tattoo often and is still considering the final design. As time has passed, I have adopted a slightly different viewpoint. Although I would rather he not get a tattoo, if he does, it will be his way of expressing his tribute, not only to me but also to the family going through this together, all the while feeling God's presence and knowing He will always be there.

> *And a woman was there who had been subject to bleeding for twelve years. She had suffered a great deal under the care of many doctors and had spent all she had, yet instead of getting better she grew worse. When she heard about Jesus, she came up behind him in the crowd and touched his cloak, because she thought, "If I just touch his clothes, I will be healed." Immediately her bleeding stopped and she felt in her body that she was freed from her suffering.*
>
> *At once Jesus realized that power had gone out from him. He turned around in the crowd and asked, "Who touched my clothes?" "You see the people crowding against you," his disciples answered, "and yet you can ask, 'Who touched me?'"*
>
> *But Jesus kept looking around to see who had done it. Then the woman, knowing what had happened to her, came and fell at his feet and, trembling with fear, told him the whole truth. He said to her, "Daughter, your faith has healed you. Go in peace and be freed from your suffering."*
> Mark 5:25–34 (NIV)

In this passage, Jesus was physically touched by the woman and felt the power leave while she knew He would heal her. She felt His presence.

> *In my former book, Theophilus, I wrote about all that Jesus began to do and to teach until the day he was taken up to heaven, after giving instructions through the Holy Spirit to the apostles he had chosen. After his suffering, he showed himself to these men and gave many convincing proofs that he was*

alive. He appeared to them over a period of forty days and spoke about the kingdom of God. On one occasion, while he was eating with them, he gave them this command: "Do not leave Jerusalem, but wait for the gift my Father promised, which you have heard me speak about. For John baptized with water, but in a few days you will be baptized with the Holy Spirit."

So when they met together, they asked him, "Lord, are you at this time going to restore the kingdom to Israel?"

He said to them: "It is not for you to know the times or dates the Father has set by his own authority. But you will receive power when the Holy Spirit comes on you; and you will be my witnesses in Jerusalem, and in all Judea and Samaria, and to the ends of the earth."

After he said this, he was taken up before their very eyes, and a cloud hid him from their sight.

They were looking intently up into the sky as he was going, when suddenly two men dressed in white stood beside them. "Men of Galilee," they said, "why do you stand here looking into the sky? This same Jesus, who has been taken from you into heaven, will come back in the same way you have seen him go into heaven." Acts 1:1–11 (NIV)

Talk about knowing when. So much is contained in this passage of Scripture. You might want to reread the passage slowly and take note of all that was said. These men, who had been among the first to hear what the risen Jesus had to say, were unexpectedly and greatly touched and forever changed. They saw Him rise into heaven and heard the angels! I don't believe for a minute that any of them anticipated all that we read about in Acts chapter 1. They were touched and changed forever!

> *Afterward Jesus appeared again to his disciples, by the Sea of Tiberias. It happened this way: Simon Peter, Thomas (called Didymus), Nathanael from Cana in Galilee, the sons of Zebedee, and two other disciples were together. "I'm going out to fish," Simon Peter told them, and they said, "We'll go with you." So they went out and got into the boat, but that night they caught nothing.*
>
> *Early in the morning, Jesus stood on the shore, but the disciples did not realize that it was Jesus.*
>
> *He called out to them, "Friends, haven't you any fish?" "No," they answered.*
>
> *He said, "Throw your net on the right side of the boat and you will find some." When they did, they were unable to haul the net in because of the large number of fish.*
>
> *Then the disciple whom Jesus loved said to Peter, "It is the Lord!" As soon as Simon Peter heard him say, "It is the Lord," he wrapped his outer garment around him (for he had taken it off) and jumped into the water. The other disciples followed in the boat, towing the net full of fish, for they were not far from shore, about a hundred yards. When they landed, they saw a fire of burning coals there with fish on it, and some bread.*
>
> *Jesus said to them, "Bring some of the fish you have just caught." Simon Peter climbed aboard and dragged the net ashore. It was full of large fish, 153, but even with so many the net was not torn. Jesus said to them, "Come and have*

> breakfast." *None of the disciples dared ask him, "Who are you?" They knew it was the Lord. Jesus came, took the bread and gave it to them, and did the same with the fish. This was now the third time Jesus appeared to his disciples after he was raised from the dead.* John 21:1–14 (NIV)

Remember, Jesus had already been crucified and buried, yet here was the resurrected Jesus when the disciples needed him. He cooked breakfast for them and ate with them. I'm sure the disciples were not expecting Jesus to appear, meeting their immediate needs. Jesus not only met their physical needs but also obviously touched them on a much deeper level. They didn't even dare to ask him who he was. Not only did this event impact the lives of those disciples who were present that day, but as we are reading this Scripture today, we are also profoundly touched by this story over two thousand years later. The effects of His touch on those disciples that day continue to reach those who are willing to reach out in faith today, and they will continue until His coming again in glory. We are touched by the eternal hand of God—pass it on!

> *One day Peter and John were going up to the temple at the time of prayer—at three in the afternoon. Now a man crippled from birth was being carried to the temple gate called Beautiful, where he was put every day to beg from those going into the temple courts. When he saw Peter and John about to enter, he asked them for money. Peter looked straight at him, as did John. Then Peter said, "Look at us!" So the man gave them his attention, expecting to get something from them.*
>
> *Then Peter said, "Silver or gold I do not have, but what I have I give you. In the name of Jesus Christ of Nazareth, walk." Taking him by the right hand, he helped him up, and instantly the man's feet and ankles became strong. He jumped to his feet and began to walk. Then he went with*

them into the temple courts, walking and jumping, and praising God. When all the people saw him walking and praising God, they recognized him as the same man who used to sit begging at the temple gate called Beautiful, and they were filled with wonder and amazement at what had happened to him. Acts 3:1–10 (NIV)

In my opinion, the words *wonder* and *amazement* don't begin to express the reactions to this passage. Imagine what the man must have felt when he was awaiting coins or food from Peter. Instead, he would walk for the first time in his life. It was a totally unexpected healing! And I can assure you it was indescribable. I had walked all my life, even danced and figure-skated, but when I was allowed to try walking again, it was as if I had never walked before. The world was new again, so I can't begin to imagine what this man, who had never walked before, felt like. Others were witnesses to the fact that he had never been able to walk and now saw him walking. The healing of this man became much larger than an act that touched just one man. In fact, in Acts 3:16 (NIV), Peter tells the onlookers, *"By faith in the name of Jesus, this man whom you see and know was made strong. It is Jesus' name and the faith that comes through him that has given this complete healing to him, as you can all see."* This man's newfound ability to walk became a testimony of faith for others to behold.

> *Some time later, Jesus went up to Jerusalem for a feast of the Jews. Now there is in Jerusalem near the Sheep Gate a pool, which in Aramaic is called Bethesda and which is surrounded by five covered colonnades. Here a great number of disabled people used to lie—the blind, the lame, the paralyzed. One who was there had been an invalid for thirty-eight years. When Jesus saw him lying there and learned that he had been in this condition for a long time, he asked him, "Do you want to get well?"*

"Sir," the invalid replied, "I have no one to help me into the pool when the water is stirred. While I am trying to get in, someone else goes down ahead of me."

Then Jesus said to him, "Get up! Pick up your mat and walk." At once the man was cured; he picked up his mat and walked. John 5:1–9a (NIV)

The man went away and told the Jews that it was Jesus who made Him well. John 5:15 (NIV)

We see the same kind of spontaneous act and experience that touches this man forever also in Acts 3:1-10 (NIV). Obviously, this was a miracle for this man, but it also reached those whom he told about what Jesus had done for him. We must be open to what Jesus does in our lives and be willing to tell others. What a blessing to all who will hear and believe!

5

THE WEIGHT WE CARRY

"Come to me, all you who are weary and burdened, and I will give you rest."
~Matthew 11:28 (NIV)

Weight. The first words that pop into my mind when I think about weight are *extra weight* and *heavy*—definitely not things I want to think about. Carrying extra weight could be a stack of heavy items or those dreaded extra pounds. Both of these were terrifying for me. With the one arm functioning normally, I could lift some things, only after the ribs healed. I learned early on that *what* I lifted was critical. Once I was able to walk, lifting anything was a definite no. The pain was instant and excruciating in both legs if I lifted something around ten pounds. But then I began to think, *What if I weighed even ten pounds more?* Perhaps I would not be able to stand at all, as I was at that moment, because of the pain brought on by the extra pounds. Therefore, if I put on more weight, it might delay my attempt to walk. Even worse, I knew that if I delayed the walking process, it would cause me to face other challenges—and on and on. You get the picture. During times like these, I was able to understand how blessings could flow!

I was limited, and I still am, as to the amount of weight I can lift. My legs will hurt at the exact site of impact. The affects continue, but so do the lessons. When I hear of someone with knee or hip pain, I know without a doubt that losing those few extra pounds would likely alleviate some of the pain. It's not an easy recommendation to accept from someone who is fairly petite, but since I experienced the issue firsthand, maybe I can help people realize the possibilities.

The emotional pain is better described as torment. I could not be there for my children at all—certainly not physically, but neither was I aware of anything going on in their lives outside of the big events, such as my son's sixteenth birthday, so absorbed was I in my own dilemma. I wanted to be at home for his birthday to make that day a wonderful memory for him, but I was not released from the hospital until the day following his birthday. So when my dear friend Bilinda brought the birthday cake to the hospital so that we could celebrate with him, I was thrilled that we could be together. That was magnificent to me. His dad took him to get his driver's license, which was a big event, and I wasn't there—but my son didn't have to lose out again because of me. Thank you, Bill and Bilinda for being there for Trey.

I felt terrible because I had agreed to be a chaperone for my daughter's trip with a group of her fellow students who were competing in San Antonio, and now I could not do that with her. They had to get a substitute—and fast. They sent me a photo from their dinner on the river walk. Seeing the photo helped me to feel as if I were part of her life again, if even for the moment.

At one point, my daughter told me she'd talked to my son's teachers when he hadn't done well on some tests right after the accident. She felt they needed to be aware of the circumstances and understand what he might be going through, and maybe they could give him some extra help. She asked her advisers to talk to his teachers and grant him some understanding. I was proud of her for watching out for her younger brother and springing into action without asking for my opinion. She simply did what she had to do. I was, and am, proud of her for taking on the burden, the extra weight of being a mom to her brother. On the other hand, I was devastated that all I could do was watch, realizing I didn't have a clue what was going on. Each of us has an extra weight to carry, and that extra weight continues. It became clear I was not capable of being in charge of my children's care. But God was—He was then and still is today!

God tells us we are not in charge of anything. It's tough to comprehend, but Jesus demonstrated this concept by teaching us lessons through parables. Sometimes God needs to be pretty direct with me. Therefore, through my physical reality, He spoke loudly, unmistakably, and undeniably to me as well as to many others. I don't have control of anything. It's a good lesson, and though it's hard to comprehend, it's absolutely obvious—even for me! I can laugh now because God actually gave me this gift years ago. Being able to laugh was a conscious decision and became a discussion I had with my kids. I told them early on that we would get through this ordeal together, but we needed to be able to laugh through it all. When we are able to look at ourselves as observers, we almost always have to smile. It's amazing that God gets anything done, since He must be rolling in laughter when he looks at all of us in our struggles down here while knowing we need only to surrender our will to Him. He stands always ready to provide us with His perfect resolutions!

There were two particular incidents during which I had to be carried physically. Both times, I needed to look at the whole picture and be willing to allow someone to carry me. Asking for or accepting help didn't come easily to me.

The first humbling incident when I allowed myself to be carried occurred when my daughter and I went to visit my sister and her family. Her son and daughter-in-law had just become the proud parents of twins. Actually, the babies were born just weeks before my accident. I was still in a wheelchair, completely unable to bear my own weight. In order to get into the house, my nephew had to concoct a way to lift the wheelchair into the house. It was a little tense, but it worked. This was yet another challenge that was to remain in my life as I knew it. I chose not to postpone the trip but to continue on with my life, albeit with many more adaptations than I'd ever imagined. There's that agonizing decision: Is it better to stay home and avoid the hassle or to impose on people in order to go? Well, I found that it was better to move forward and do all I could and to allow others to help carry the load.

One of the most humbling experiences was when my daughter was going off to college. I was unable to bear weight on my left leg, even in a full boot. I attempted to walk with a walker, but by then, my challenges were a bit different. Since my shoulder was still painful, it was uncomfortable to use a walker with one foot, and it certainly wasn't fast. So as we began the process of unpacking the car, my family all stood still for a moment, looking at me. Eventually, my husband asked if he could carry me up the stairs. His plan was to put me on my daughter's dorm-room bed so that I could help her unpack. With the car unloaded, the guys went off for a day of golfing. Unpacking went rather smoothly, but all the while, I felt terrible that I could not get up and help Kami put things away.

Her new roommate showed up shortly after we arrived. Moms, dads, and excited, nervous students filled the hallways, scurrying up and down the staircase, in and out of every room. We enjoyed getting to know one another and deciding who got which dresser. Once both girls were sufficiently unpacked, we decided to get something to eat and relax a bit. Then reality struck. Remember, the hallways and stairwells were filled with new students and parents—and they were still there. While trying to proceed out of the room, down the hall, and down the stairs, I realized it was next to impossible for me to maneuver my walker, using one leg and one arm, down the narrow, crowded stairway. As the line of anxious students and parents collected behind me, the father of Kami's roommate looked at me and then at his wife and back to me. Hesitantly, he asked if he could carry me down the stairs. I don't remember ever before saying yes to help that quickly! Although it was embarrassing to be a grown woman slung over some man's shoulder, especially a man I had barely met, my only thought at the time was to get down those stairs and to facilitate the movement of those anxious folks behind me. This gentleman carried some extra weight for sure, yet I released some inhibitions that day by beginning to realize I could and should ask for or accept help from the wonderful people who offered it.

That brings me back to the weight we carry, both literally and figuratively. Sometimes weight is literal, as it was for me during that time. In that scenario, weight meant pounds. But the weight I *didn't* carry was what amazed me. I looked at people's faces while they listened to the accident details or saw my physical challenges. Some were weighed down with despair and questions about how something like this could happen. But that was just it! It's not as if I don't—or won't—ever face spiritual challenges, but I didn't then. I knew I would be okay, although I didn't know exactly what "okay" would mean at that time. I didn't struggle with or ponder that at all. I didn't know when this trial would be over—I just knew it would be! Looking back on that time now, I remember that people actually told me, to my face, that they wished they had my faith. I struggled with that reality. I have always had deep faith that God was present to guide us wherever and whenever we needed Him. I am comfortable that everything that happens is for a specific reason—maybe we will see why, and maybe we will never know, but that isn't something I ever questioned. I consider this yet another amazing blessing from God that I didn't intend to have tested, but it was obviously according to God's will.

I recently heard Mary Beth Chapman discuss some things that I have struggled to put into words for four years. She said, "I just hope that I can steward this message well." She was referring to seeing why God allowed such a terrible tragedy in the Chapman family. She knew her little girl was not coming back, and the nightmare of losing a child would never be turned around, but she also knew and was comforted by the knowledge that this was, in fact, God's plan. Something awesome would come out of this heartache. Although she didn't know what or when it was to come, in her heart of hearts, she knew that there would someday come a time when God's message would be heard—through her. I understood that kind of struggle. I knew I needed to share the passion that God had instilled in me about who He is and what our faith in Him can accomplish.

I remember answering that oh-so-poignant question: "Don't you wonder why this happened to you?" I was stunned. Why, no! I didn't waste my time wondering why, because I already knew. There was some way I was to use this series of events that I now know as a series of miracles. I knew all I wanted to do was steward this message well. And with God's help, this is what I will do, now or whenever—it is in His time. The things I could do were to channel all my energy into laughter about myself with my kids and enjoy what interesting new little thing I could accomplish in each day I was given. Heck, I was thrilled to be able to dial the phone. My thumb hurt. It took three months to be able to use that thumb to dial my cell phone! I texted a photo of both shoes on the day I was allowed to stand with full weight on both legs! Ain't life grand?

There was an evening early on, when three friends of ours came to visit. The air seemed somewhat heavy and stagnant. My husband had surgery just days after I arrived back home. The surgery had been previously scheduled, and we chose not to delay it. These gentlemen wanted to be there for both of us, but it became obvious they were completely overwhelmed by the needs of our household.

One friend came over to me as I was proudly propped up in the corner of the couch, pillows supporting every limb. He leaned down and, with sincerity, asked, "How are you ever going to get through this?" I was surprised but immediately reassured him that I *would* get through this. There was no doubt in my mind about that, I told him, but I also knew I would face added struggles if I put on any weight while in the wheelchair. He couldn't believe his ears. He thought that was an odd thing for me to say. It was the honest truth. Although I was physically pretty broken, I still thought like a woman. I knew I would get through this, but putting on weight would devastate me. I felt that would be too much weight for me to bear. And you might be able to guess what's coming next.

The day I was allowed to bear my full weight standing on both feet, I stepped on the scale, as any other woman would. I weighed exactly the same as the day I had flipped! My weight was certainly rearranged, but I weighed the same. I thanked God that my weight had remained stable while I was wheelchair-bound, but then the weight challenge began. Yes, I did gain some weight, but not much. At about the three-year mark, I began to get uncomfortable in my own clothes. I knew my limitations, so I didn't carry a lot of things. I didn't overdo anything but eating. I am a nervous eater. So as I began to experience my limitations, albeit with acceptance, reality was a rude intruder. Although I graciously accept what I can and cannot do, I have moments of reflection on some abilities lost. Between refraining from lifting and carrying and the frustrations of having to ask for help, I tend to grab stuff to munch on. That certainly doesn't help. Now I face every woman's ultimate challenge: I can't find anything to wear!

So I try to focus on times of solitude, both within myself and with God. Will you also allow Him to guide you into knowing who you truly are? It is important, for me at least, to understand how I work so that I can become a better servant. I am a happy person, driven to try to make others happy and to share. I love to listen and learn, but I also love to teach. If I am uncomfortable, it becomes difficult to listen, learn, or share. For me, basic comfort means being physically fit and feeling well, as well as feeling good about myself. Therefore, weight was a distracting issue for me. My physical weight gain made the emotional weight unbearable. After acknowledging this as me, I am trying to lose the weight in order to feel good about myself. Then I can give tenfold and share, listen, and care for others. God helps me realize how I work. He is the source of my strength to address my work, and He helps me carry the weight I bear.

I believe we all have challenges, and those become the weight we carry. There was one weight I carried for over ten years before I realized it. I had been to a weekend retreat at an older conference center that had a musty smell. I had been dealing with a bizarre muscle reaction for years. If my senses were overwhelmed, my muscles would tremor. This musty smell triggered this reaction. Since I was at the conference center for a long weekend, my sense of smell was overwhelmed for days without any relief, so the tremors increased in the number of occurrences and in severity. They were minimal at first, and no one noticed. I could manage, but then it became uncontrollable. I stepped out of a small group into the hallway, where I lost all control. One of the facilitators noticed when I left the group and followed me out. He undoubtedly could see that I was having some kind of problem, so I had to explain that this was part of my life. I had been dealing with these muscle tremors for years. The doctors could not agree on any diagnosis. I was given all kinds of medications over several years, but nothing seemed to help. Eventually, I had a surgery that did reduce them. This was followed up with some other medical processes, but the problem never completely went away. The doctors were just as frustrated as I that there seemed to be no cure. I stopped pursuing an answer, since it didn't happen often enough to be a real concern. But at this retreat, the problem became terrifying, because now it had happened in public, and others were watching. I was embarrassed, frustrated, and hurting inside and out.

Shortly, several people streamed out of the meeting to be with me. They assembled a prayer team but were mindful not to disrupt the retreat activities for everyone else. The spiritual director for the weekend was a delightful priest I had not met before. He stayed with me while the others went into the meeting room to arrange for a prayer team during the next break.

We sat together, not knowing what to say, until Father Steve looked at me and asked if I had ever asked God to take this issue away. Being in the midst of tremors and struggling to concentrate on controlling what muscles I could, I couldn't even begin to comprehend my own embarrassment. I answered from my heart: "How could I ask God to take this away? Haven't I had enough blessings and miracles in my life?" Father Steve was speechless. The honesty of my questions seemed to take him back for a moment. After all, my response did seem logical, if only for a moment. On the other hand, I realized how dumb that reasoning sounded. Who was I to judge that I had hit some sort of a blessing limit with God? At that moment, I knew I needed to give that burden to God. I had been carrying a tremendous weight that I was not meant to carry. I am sure God allowed that experience to happen with those people surrounding me at that moment in order for me to finally see that it was not up to me. I needed to relinquish the heavy burden of the tremors—along with all the decisions as to when, where, and how to pursue the strange reaction—into God's hands. And I have. I heard God tell me that it was time to pursue my health and all that involved.

Eventually, I became willing to be led by God and was able to see His paths unveiled before me. I found a neurologist, and although he admitted I was a challenge, my family and I felt comfortable that he understood, at least in part, what was happening. So a year after that weekend experience, I was comforted by looking back and seeing God's ability to lead me when I had given my burdens to Him. I had needlessly carried a burden that I should have given to Him long before. How often do we carry these extra weights needlessly? Once I recognized my shortsightedness and handed the weight over to God, I found direction.

Soon I will be going back to another of these weekend retreats, this time as a staff member, praying that I will be given the words to help others understand how God is calling them to serve Him and that these words will be received with open hearts.

> *"Come to me, all you who are weary and burdened and I will give you rest. Take my yoke upon you and learn from me, for I am gentle and humble in heart, and you will find rest for your souls. For my yoke is easy and my burden is light."* Matthew 11:28–30 (NIV)

> *Praise be to the Lord, to God our Savior, who daily bears our burdens.* Psalm 68:19 (NIV)

> *So the soldiers took charge of Jesus. Carrying his own cross, he went out to the place of the Skull (which in Aramaic is called Golgotha). Here they crucified him, and with him two others—one on each side and Jesus in the middle.* John 19:16b–18 (NIV)

Undeniably, we see Jesus physically carrying His cross in this passage of Scripture. Take a moment to reflect on this scene, realizing that He carried not only the physical weight of the cross but also the weight of the sins of the whole world. He did this to atone for my sin and yours.

There are Scripture references below, plus many others not included here, that tell of how Jesus carried our burdens to the cross. How many times has He taken yours?

> *The rabble with them began to crave other food, and again the Israelites started wailing and said, "If only we had meat to eat! We remember the fish we ate in Egypt at no cost— also the cucumbers, melons, leeks, onions and garlic. But now we have lost our appetite; we never see anything but this manna!"*
>
> *The manna was like coriander seed and looked like resin. The people went around gathering it, and then ground it in a handmill or crushed it in a mortar. They cooked it in a pot or made it into cakes. And it tasted like something made with olive oil. When the dew settled on the camp at night, the manna also came down.*
>
> *Moses heard the people of every family wailing, each at the entrance to his tent. The LORD became exceedingly angry, and Moses was troubled. He asked the LORD, "Why have you brought this trouble on your servant? What have I done to displease you that you put the burden of all these people on me? Did I conceive all these people? Did I give them birth?"*
> Numbers 11:4–17 (NIV)
>
> *Shout with joy to God, all the earth!*
> *Sing the glory of his name;*
> *make his praise glorious!*
> *Say to God, "How awesome are your deeds!*
> *So great is your power*
> *that your enemies cringe before you.*
> *All the earth bows down to you;*
> *they sing praise to you,*

they sing praise to your name."
Come and see what God has done,
how awesome his works in man's behalf!
He turned the sea into dry land,
they passed through the waters on foot—
come, let us rejoice in him.
He rules forever by his power,
his eyes watch the nations—
let not the rebellious rise up against him.
Praise our God, O peoples,
let the sound of his praise be heard;
he has preserved our lives
and kept our feet from slipping.
For you, O God, tested us;
you refined us like silver.
You brought us into prison
and laid burdens on our backs.
You let men ride over our heads;
we went through fire and water,
but you brought us to a place of abundance.
I will come to your temple with burnt offerings
and fulfill my vows to you—
vows my lips promised and my mouth spoke
when I was in trouble.
I will sacrifice fat animals to you
and an offering of rams;
I will offer bulls and goats
.Come and listen, all you who fear God;
let me tell you what he has done for me.
I cried out to him with my mouth;
his praise was on my tongue.
If I had cherished sin in my heart,
the Lord would not have listened;
but God has surely listened

and heard my voice in prayer.
Praise be to God,
who has not rejected my prayer
or withheld his love from me! Psalm 66:1–20 (NIV)

I love this Psalm. It talks about burdens, but it also conveys an excitement in living a godly life—one in which we give glory to God and attempt to put the focus on Him and on giving back to Him in order to honor Him.

Praise be to the Lord, to God our Savior,
who daily bears our burdens.
Our God is a God who saves;
from the Sovereign LORD comes escape from
death. Psalm 68:19–20 (NIV)

This verse is short but poignant. God does bear our daily burdens. Some He carries, and some we make a conscious effort to give to Him. The second verse goes immediately to the ultimate reality: God not only carries our burdens but also has provided us with an "escape from death." We just need to accept Him as our Lord and Savior and give Him all our burdens. This is amazing! It seems so simple. By my sharing some of my experiences and having my own eyes, heart, and mind opened, I hope you will also come to the realization that giving everything to God must become a conscious effort. As you become aware of circumstances, worries, choices, and aha moments in your own life, give them all to God. We must be willing to surrender them all to God's tender care.

I expect this to be a lifelong journey. As much as I would like to think I could easily and continually give all my cares and worries into God's keeping, I have chosen to focus not on how well I do this but on the act of continuing to do it better.

> *Sing for joy to God our strength;*
> *shout aloud to the God of Jacob!*
> *Begin the music, strike the tambourine,*
> *play the melodious harp and lyre.*
> *Sound the ram's horn at the New Moon,*
> *and when the moon is full, on the day of our Feast;*
> *This is the decree of Israel,*
> *an ordinance of the God of Jacob.*
> *He established it as a statute for Joseph*
> *he went out against Egypt,*
> *we heard a language that we did not understand.*
> *He says, "I removed the burden from their shoulders;*
> *their hands were set free from the basket.*
> *In your distress you called and I rescued you,*
> *I answered you out of a thundercloud;*
> *I tested you at the waters of Meribah."* Psalm 81:1–7 (NIV)

As I looked for verses that focused on burdens and God's asking us to lay our burdens down and turn them over to Him, I often saw another scene emerging. In the Bible, just before we hear His directive or hear Him say He will take our burdens, the passage seems to be one of gleeful celebration. It often seems a good time to point out the difficulties, when one is focused on the joys life has to offer. This can be an effective teaching moment. It is true that we rarely see the blessings, great or small, during a hardship, until He points them out to us or sends someone to us to point them out for us. Then we can once again strive to open our eyes and hearts to see all the joys He has placed there for us to see and feel.

> *I, the teacher, was king over Israel in Jerusalem. I devoted myself to study and to explore by wisdom all that is done under heaven. What a heavy burden God has laid on men! I have seen all the things that are done under the sun; all of them are meaningless, a chasing after the wind.*

*What is twisted cannot be straightened;
what is lacking cannot be counted.*

I thought to myself, "Look, I have grown and increased in wisdom more than anyone who has ruled over Jerusalem before me; I have experienced much wisdom and knowledge." Then I applied myself to the understanding of wisdom, and also of madness and folly, but I learned that this, too, is a chasing after the wind.

For with much wisdom comes much sorrow; the more knowledge, the more grief. Ecclesiastes 1:12–18 (NIV)

To me, the above passage from Ecclesiastes shows an entirely different perspective regarding burdens. When we strive to live as God has shown us, to live by His Word, a life of obedience and sharing with others, we see a different kind of burden because of our increased wisdom and knowledge.

When you think about it, this is how it is in corporate America. You want that next promotion, that new responsibility, and that larger paycheck, of course. But what really happens? With that new title, recognition, responsibility, and money comes a whole new set of responsibilities—yes, burdens! Things don't actually get any easier in the corporate world or even in life in general. Sure, some things might seem easier, but how many of us recite the statement "If I only knew then what I know now"? Yes, this knowledge is a burden. We ache to share what we have learned with those who are younger and less experienced so that they can avoid the pain of our own mistakes and make better choices.

I don't know about you, but I never thought of wisdom as a burden, especially since we all like to think of wisdom and knowledge as accomplishments. But along with accomplishments come responsibilities, and doesn't that added responsibility become burdensome at times?

> *Yet you have not called upon me, O Jacob,*
> *you have not wearied yourselves for me, O Israel.*
> *You have not brought me sheep for burnt offerings,*
> *nor honored me with your sacrifices.*
> *I have not burdened you with grain offerings*
> *nor wearied you with demands for incense.*
> *You have not bought any fragrant calamus for me,*
> *or lavished on me the fat of your sacrifices.*
> *But you have burdened me with your sins and wearied me*
> *with your offenses.*
> *I, even I, am he who blots out*
> *your transgressions, for my own sake,*
> *and remembers your sins no more.* Isaiah 43:22–28 (NIV)

Here is a verse with a different view on burdens. Here, *we* burden God. It is the essence of what we don't want to do, yet we do it. But God asks us to lay our burdens on Him. So how is this different? I believe the difference lies within our hearts. How did we burden God? Did we earnestly ask Him to take our burdens so that we could move forward with Him, guided by Him on His path for us, or did we ignore what He taught us in the Scriptures, thus leaving Him burdened with our unbelief?

Taking this burden in its full context creates a scene of joy and glory whereby God recognizes that some burdens could easily get in the way of our celebrating all He has to offer. I believe this is what God has been trying to show us in many ways. We should give Him our burdens, enjoy all He has provided for us, envelope ourselves in His Word, live it, and share it. It's hard to look at any single concept of this word *burden*. Most artists will tell you to look at the whole picture—not just the individual brushstrokes or colors, but the entire picture as a whole. The pieces of God's plan fit together perfectly as a unit, yet we can't grasp the whole until it is complete. There are times when a picture becomes more apparent midway through the process, but the best view takes time to be completed and must be studied after completion.

Does any of this help you to grasp how God explains that our understanding—much like our view of a painting in progress—is limited? However, when we look back over our lives, we are amazed at how God's hand was there throughout it all. Sometimes we can smile through this process, while at other times, we can't see that it will ever come out right. Just believe!

> *Now we know that if the earthly tent we live in is destroyed, we have a building from God, an eternal house in heaven, not built by human hands. Meanwhile we groan, longing to be clothed with our heavenly dwelling, because when we are clothed, we will not be found naked. For while we are in this tent, we groan and are burdened, because we do not wish to be unclothed but to be clothed with our heavenly dwelling, so that what is mortal may be swallowed up by life. Now it is God who has made us for this very purpose and has given us the Spirit as a deposit, guaranteeing what is to come.*
>
> *Therefore we are always confident and know that as long as we are at home in the body we are away from the Lord, we live by faith, not by sight.* 2 Corinthians 5:1–7 (NIV)

Again, we see a slightly different meaning of a burden. Here, *we* are burdened with a heavy heart longing to be in heaven. So there is no particular physical issue at hand, but there is one imposed by wisdom from the Word. Heaven awaits!

> *Brothers, if someone is caught in a sin, you who are spiritual should restore him gently. But watch yourself, or you also may be tempted. Carry each other's burdens, and in this way you will fulfill the law of Christ. If anyone thinks he is something when he is nothing, he deceives himself. Each*

> *one should test his own actions. Then he can take pride in himself, without comparing himself to somebody else, for each one should carry his own load.*
>
> *Anyone who receives instruction in the work must share all good things with his instructor.* Galatians 6:1–6 (NIV)

For the first time, we see burdens also as the responsibility of others here on Earth. There is a reference to "someone else" and to "his instructor." God tells us to "share all the good things." So are we seeing a contradiction in His directions? I think not! We are to give Him our burdens so that we can continue to study His work and accept His directions for our lives, but we must also take responsibility for our own actions. He did give us a brain, after all, and instructed us to use what He has given us. We need to first be aware of what it is that burdens us and then work to resolve it. Sometimes that becomes a long process. At other times, it requires discussion or just dumping our problems on a friend. How often do your problems seem less severe after you tell someone else? I think this is the intent here: we should resolve the problems we can but hand whatever becomes greater than a problem—a true burden—over to God.

In summary, we will always carry all kinds of weight: pounds, troubles, burdens of decision or indecision, and heartache. These will always abound until He brings us home. This last biblical reference sums it up for me. I hope it helps you too. Whatever is weighing you down, hand it to God in faith, believing.

> *Everyone who believes that Jesus is the Christ is born of God, and everyone who loves the father loves his child as well. This is how we know that we love the children of God: by loving God and carrying out his commands. This is love for God: to obey his commands. And his commands are not burdensome, for everyone born of God overcomes the world. This is the*

victory that has overcome the world, even our faith. Who is it that overcomes the world? Only he who believes that Jesus is the Son of God. 1 John 5:1–5 (NIV)

6

RECONSTRUCTION— NEW CREATION

"Therefore, if anyone is in Christ, he is a new creation;
the old has gone, and the new has come!"
~2 Corinthians 5:17 (NIV)

When you are physically injured and someone says the word *reconstruction*, you automatically think of physical reconstructions. Indeed, there were many physical reconstructions in my journey, but the emotional and spiritual reconstructions are the much bigger story!

Both of my legs were crushed in the car accident. Displacement of the kneecaps was required in order to insert metal rods into each leg to hold the bones in place. There were screws at the top and the bottom to anchor each rod in place, as well as a long line of staples in each kneecap.

My right ankle was completely shattered. I can imagine the surgeon trying to grab my ankle and hold it together while anchoring it in place. It must have looked much like watching someone gather tissue paper around a bottle and hold on to it while quickly tying the ribbon on the top to hold it together, all the while hoping it will look nice when it's done! A plate was inserted to hold the outside of the ankle together. One could actually see all five screw heads. Then they put a long nail through the bottom of my foot. I am sure it was just for good measure! As I looked at the x-rays, it almost looked as if the nail were an afterthought: "Let's just put a nail in here to make sure it all stays together!"

In addition to the fact that nothing in my life was routine, I had hairy legs. Yes, the hair on my legs grew back, and I had to shave them. As I eased over the right leg, which had minimal reconstruction, I would nick the five ankle screws while shaving. Shaving was something else to overcome. Couldn't God at least keep the hair from growing back on my legs? Not only did I have to shave my legs over the screws and broken bone bumps, but also, I had to shave (and early on, I might add) over the skin graft on my thigh. The surgeons had to take my own skin to rebuild not only the inside of my left leg but also the outside. Talk about a complete teardown!

When I finally got to see these x-rays, I saw what I thought were a lot of stitches. Actually, they were tiny staples constricting each vein and artery, since much of the inside of the leg was taken out permanently. Many of the other broken bones were better left alone. So left to heal on their own were eight ribs, a shoulder, and a collapsed lung. Then I learned, about three years later, that my foot had been broken in the accident but likely not fixed at the time, since the injury hadn't been life-threatening. But here was the stark reality: this process would not be over when I left the hospital. I would have reconstructive surgeries for years, fixing one thing after another. I did not deliberately set out to rebuild my body or my life or to consciously assess what I needed to deal with in order to move forward, but looking back, I realize that in many ways, my reconstruction was not just surgical.

I felt compelled to write a tribute to my rescue teams. I wanted to meet the firefighters and paramedics who had been there at the scene. I talked to the officer on duty when I was in the hospital, but I wanted to talk to him again, to show him how I had not only survived but was also rebuilt physically with amazing capabilities, far exceeding anyone's expectations. I also wanted to share my spiritual growth through all that had happened.

I felt immediate comfort in meeting and connecting with some of my rescue teams. It took a period of time for me to fully understand how meeting these people had contributed to my own reconstruction and the rebuilding of my life into what it is now. Like renovating an ancient structure, reconstruction takes time. Although it is planned and takes many people diligently working toward the same goal, it is only through the passage of time that we begin to see the new structure emerging. Often, the original plans must be changed in order to enhance the new structure! After the fact, we can sometimes see that some things that were completely unplanned made a huge difference in the outcome, such as my being able to meet with these teams. I never really thought about it as being a part of my recovery and closing the gap. Being able to share all my successes with those who, at least here on Earth, made it all possible was an important step. Many of the architects and builders of those ancient structures didn't live to see the outcomes. Like them, we will likely never see the final version of our own transformation in this life. You see, we never reach completion, at least not here on Earth. Our decision to live a godly life requires altering our behavior and decision-making processes so that they always include Him. We must make time to listen for His direction as we continually grow and change. Our spiritual growth process never stops. I believe part of the building and restructuring process is to take a look back to where we were, see what stands firm today, and then decide what we might need to focus on in order to build our lives in accordance with His will.

As in any construction or reconstruction project, the focus must be on the plans and what needs to be happening at any given time in order to carry those plans to completion. Interruptions are not welcome. I did not have the luxury of a written set of plans for returning to a normal life. I was blessed to take each day, and often each moment, at a time and accept it for the blessing it was and to celebrate the joy in each little accomplishment. Since there were many things that kept my life from being anywhere near normal, I did what I was told for the physical concerns and forged ahead with God's guidance and His still, small voice within.

After all, I was a mom. My heart was yearning to be there for my children. I also knew with every substance of my being that I would not do anything to risk my long-term physical recovery for any kind of short-term gain. I have no doubt that God had a hand or a voice in everything I did. Of course, things didn't always go as planned. I have come to realize that God allowed me to make the change from a demanding, structured corporate lifestyle to that of a real-estate agent, a career in which not a moment is planned, and even when you think it is, rest assured that your plan will be rearranged. Therefore, my career set the stage—I was already accustomed to ever-changing plans, readjusting time and space, and living moment to moment. So when an obstacle came my way, God had already prepared me to alter my course and take things as they came. It didn't even occur to me to label changes in plans as obstacles, which was a blessing. He had helped me make that adjustment already, so I didn't struggle with change; it had already become a way of life!

One thing I was immediately thankful for was that this accident had happened to me rather than to either of my children. I kept this thought close to my heart with incredible gratitude. As hard as life was for me, not only physically but also financially and in terms of overall uncertainties about my future, I didn't have to see this experience through the eyes of a parent watching her child suffer. In fact, one of my deepest heartaches was watching my children have to cope with life as it was, but it was my physical abilities, not theirs, that were permanently altered. I felt that they would get past this time and be able to live normal lives, and that was my prayer.

But it struck me that although I was a grown woman with a family, I was also someone's child. My parents were still alive, although they were getting on in years. They were unable to travel, so they had to rely on only what they were told. They suspected they were being shielded from the full extent of the devastation. With this realization, I wanted to see my parents and show them how well I was doing—and so it was. My daughter and sister arranged for a flight to North Carolina for me to see my parents. I was still in wheelchair, so we planned how and where to meet them, because there would be no one there able to lift my wheelchair into their home.

Once again, God intervened. Two days before we were to leave, my doctor allowed me to use a walker. It was not fun—it was painful, in fact—because I could use only one arm and one leg, but I felt it might be enough to allow me to get into my parents' home. Being able to visit them in their home was important to me, because I had seen many people's faces reveal disbelief and heartache for me when they first saw me. I didn't want my parents' first view of me to be in a public place. As a parent myself, I didn't think that would be fair to them. Using the walker, I was able to scooch up the few steps into their sunroom and then into the house. It felt awesome! I got to show them not only that I had survived but also that my life would carry on. I was blessed no matter how I looked at it, and they saw that firsthand. Once they got over the initial shock, they also saw the joy in my life and not just the destruction.

While I was in the hospital, I overheard a rather frantic discussion. The discussion involved yet another, possibly unpleasant, reconstruction surgery and an attempt to avoid it by reassessing the need on an hour-to-hour basis.

Several days after the accident, my body seemed to decide it had had enough. My bodily functions were shutting down. The physical trauma of the suffering the injuries, undergoing several surgeries, and being under anesthesia for many hours of reconstructive surgeries had taken its toll. I was immobile, except for being moved in and out of surgery. My colon had stopped working. I remember being incredibly uncomfortable and irritable—not in the areas related to the injuries or surgeries so much, but in my midsection. Dr. James H. "Red" Duke Jr., head of the trauma unit, was the physician leading the team. He was growing more and more concerned that they would have to intervene surgically to relieve the distress.

I knew from others who had been through similar surgeries that this could be potentially life-altering (not that everything else wasn't already). The surgery they were contemplating could require me to wear a bag for the rest of my life. I could not bear the thought of having to deal with something else.

My dear friend Bilinda once again called for prayers that this issue would work itself out without surgical intervention. She begged him to reconsider. At her pleading, the doctor agreed to hold off on the surgery, but he would require x-rays every hour on the hour to assess the situation. This issue was not a result of the physical damage incurred in the accident; rather, it was one of the effects of constant medication and physical immobility. I felt there must be some way to stimulate the colon back to working order. At that, the doctor took a moment to contemplate possible alternatives. He then recalled there was one old, natural remedy that might work. He asked if I was willing to try. He didn't have to ask me twice! Therefore, the new regimen began. Eventually, I was restored to full health, at least for that particular body part.

Sometimes starting over completely seemed to be the best option. Speaking from the perspective of the physical reconstructions I had already endured, starting over with a whole new body would have been an exciting thought. Of course, that's not an option this side of heaven, but sometimes things can be made new again from a different starting point.

> *The LORD said to Moses, "Chisel out two stone tablets like the first ones, and I will write on them the words that were on the first tablets, which you broke."* Exodus 34:1 (NIV)

How often do we wish we could start over? When things break or when it becomes obvious that we have made wrong choices, we wish we could have a do-over. When we don't get the chance to start over, we must reconstruct from the brokenness.

I think God must have said something like this to the firefighters, paramedics, and doctors attending me that day: "Don't worry about the process of rebuilding. Work with what you are presented in the moment, and begin to rebuild; then reassess as you go along." They all did things they had never done before or thought possible from the initial rescue process in an attempt to put me back together in whatever form or fashion that might be. Now I amazed at what He helped them create! They rebuilt what they could and hoped for the best. Many prayed, and God answered those prayers to a degree that none of us could have ever imagined.

It astonishes me to think of something as sacred as the stone tablets upon which God Himself wrote out the Ten Commandments and to then realize that the tablets that were carried in the Ark of the Covenant were reconstructed! How often do we look at people or objects yet never know the reconstruction—physically or spiritually—that has taken place in their lives? Have you ever considered what might have caused you to change your path, good or bad? Or what caused you to focus more intensely on your spiritual path? It's interesting to contemplate, isn't it?

That's the beauty of reconstruction. Sometimes we don't even realize anything was different. We rarely recognize the subtle beginning of our ever-changing heart and soul.

God works that way too. People you meet usually accept you based on their perceptions of you at the time you meet. They might spend time getting to know you better and might even learn about some of your past, but I don't know anyone who focuses on your entire journey. The relationship is usually based on who you are today. That tells me a lot about what God is asking us to do. Let's assess our spiritual path and reconstruct as necessary. It doesn't matter where we have been before the reconstruction. What matters is the path we are building now.

> *For I am the LORD, your God,*
> *who takes hold of your right hand*
> *and says to you, "Do not fear;*
> *I will help you.*
> *Do not be afraid, O worm Jacob,*
> *O little Israel,*
> *for I myself will help you," declares the LORD,*
> *your Redeemer, the Holy One of Israel.*
> *"See, I will make you into a threshing sledge,*
> *new and sharp, with many teeth.*
> *You will thresh the mountains and crush them,*
> *and reduce the hills to chaff.*
> *You will winnow them, the wind will pick them up,*
> *and a gale will blow them away.*
> *But you will rejoice in the LORD*
> *and glory in the Holy One of Israel."* Isaiah 41:13–16 (NIV)

For me, this is an awesome passage of Scripture, showing how God offers assurance of who He is and promises that He will be right there. He commits to helping us and making us into something new—something better and stronger than before, with capabilities far beyond our imagination. Then He reminds us specifically to give the glory to Him. That's pretty straightforward, yet when we look at anything that's been rebuilt or reconstructed or is a work in progress, do we stand back and enjoy the finished product *before* we recognize that God's hand was in each and every step? Think about it. Could this be part of what you need to reconstruct—taking in the beauty along the way?

> *The king should know that we went to the district of Judah, to the temple of the great God. The people are building it with large stones and placing the timbers in the walls. The work is being carried on with diligence and is making rapid progress under their direction.*
>
> *We questioned the elders and asked them, "Who authorized you to rebuild this temple and restore this structure?" We also asked them their names, so that we could write down the names of their leaders for your information.*
>
> *This is the answer they gave us:*
>
> *"We are servants of the God of heaven and earth, and we are rebuilding the temple that was built many years ago, one that a great king of Israel built and finished. But because our fathers angered the God of heaven, he handed them over to Nebuchadnezzar the Chaldean, king of Babylon, who destroyed this temple and deported the people Babylon."*
>
> *"However, in the first year of Cyrus king of Babylon, King Cyrus issued a decree to rebuild this house of God. He even removed from the temple of Babylon the gold and silver articles of the house of God, which Nebuchadnezzar had*

> *taken from the temple of Jerusalem and brought to the temple in Babylon. Then King Cyprus gave them to a man named Sheshbazzar, whom he had appointed govenor, and he told him, 'Take these articles and go and deposit them in the temple in Jerusalem. And rebuild the house of God on its site.' So this Sheshbazzar came and laid the foundations of the house of God in Jerusalem. From that day to the present it has been under construction but is not yet finished."*
> Ezra 5:8–16 (NIV)

Reread this passage. It is amazing. This is what God says about us and the world we live in. This passage is the same directive, just specific to a temple built for God, allowed to be destroyed because of disobedience. Then He commanded it to be rebuilt in His time. He does exactly what He says He will do if we don't obey. Rebuild your life in His name for His purpose, and He will reward you in heaven.

> *Create in me a pure heart, O God,*
> *and renew a steadfast spirit within me.*
> *Do not cast me from your presence*
> *or take your Holy Spirit from me.*
> *Restore in me the joy of your salvation*
> *and grant me a willing spirit, to sustain me.*
> Psalm 51:10–12 (NIV)

While the focus here is on restoration and reconstruction rather than on focusing on the suffering and dread of what we often feel that process will entail, the passage dwells on the joy of what the outcome will be—expressed with excitement and anticipation. I think this attitude toward making a change—making it with anticipation—is, in and of itself, a major change. Keeping this in mind—positioning your heart in humility, not in pretense—allows you to experience joy and thankfulness to a much greater extent. I believe a humble approach to life keeps your heart and mind open.

It is the beginning of accepting, learning, and yearning for more of what God has offered to us. I also think that living in humility can help us get through the reconstruction.

We must recognize that we are not reconstructing and are not in control; we are blessed to be allowed to choose to follow His Word and do whatever it takes. If you humble yourself as you encounter major obstacles, you will alleviate the obstacles you put in your own path.

Accept what needs to be done, and do it graciously. Focus on what is to come and not on how long it will take or on the hardships required to get there. Reconstruction takes on many forms. Again, here's something we need to seriously ponder and then put into action: a positive outlook makes the uglies a lot easier to take.

Only in recapping some of the things I went through could I see and begin to express all the heartache that I *didn't* have to experience, simply because He had either taken it away completely or had taught me to accept it, move forward, look for the silver lining, and laugh.

These are seemingly small and insignificant gifts—yes, I said gifts! I do not consider them talents but true blessings. They continue to help me see everything in my life as a blessing. Even the tough stuff has a silver lining when we are willing to look for it. God has created and offered the world to us if we only take the time to view it as such.

7

A GLIMPSE OF WHAT AWAITS

"[God] called you out of darkness into his wonderful light."
~1 Peter 2:9b (NIV)

We are taught as children that we will go to heaven someday. Some people say things such as "It's a glorious place" or "You have to be good to get to heaven." The Scriptures have much more to say about how to get to heaven and what it will be like. Everything goes back to reading the Word. Almost as important for me as reading the Scriptures is studying and sharing God's Word with others. Sharing His Word helps us learn to live the lives God has planned for us. Sometimes I also find it comforting—and amazing—to read or hear of others who have actually experienced heaven. Some examples of personal testimonies are Don Piper, who wrote *90 Minutes in Heaven*, or the book entitled *Heaven Is for Real*, written by Todd Burpo with Lynn Vincent, about a four-year-old boy named Colton, who experienced heaven. Another example is the story of Freddie Vest, the Texas rodeo cowboy who died and experienced being in the Lord's presence before returning to this life.

On the Friday evening after the accident, March 31, I struggled with an experience of my own. I had had hours of surgeries during the week to reconstruct both legs. Rods were inserted to stabilize the bones in each leg, and I had additional surgeries to begin the reconstruction of the left leg, which would eventually be rebuilt using my own muscle and skin. Several skilled surgeons worked many hours that Friday evening to complete their surgical plan. Then we had to wait to see how my body responded. Would my body accept my legs and regenerate the bones? Or would the body reject them, in which case I would lose them?

My eighteen-year-old daughter, Kami, was at my bedside. She wanted to be there with me and to help in any way she could. I was touched and welcomed her nearness. There seemed to be a flurry of activity in the recovery room. The nurses were stressed. They attempted to put an oxygen mask on my face and secure it with the strap around my head. I was completely aware of what was going on but couldn't communicate well.

They were placing the strap across the gash in the back of my head. During the week, I had repeatedly said that there was something in my head. The nurses would examine the gash and tell me that a portion of it was superficial, while some of the gash was a bit deeper, but they said not to worry. Well, it hurt, but since I was not able to verbalize that the strap was hurting the cut in my head, I began to flail my arms, pushing the mask away. The nurse shot my daughter a look of dismay and frustration, as I appeared to be uncooperative. Kami explained to the nurse that I have never liked things on my face. By then, the nurse was getting angry. She was adamant that I needed the oxygen right then or they would have to intubate me. I was not sure what that process would entail, but I knew it was not a step in the right direction. So Kami asked the nurse if she could stand there and hold the oxygen mask on my face. I was heartbroken to see my daughter standing by my side while I lay helpless. I didn't want her to have to go through this. And then I left.

I remember the experience vividly. I left. I started to recite the Serenity Prayer and stumbled over some of the words. I couldn't get it right, and then I knew He would understand. I felt myself let go of my own thoughts, and I was cradled in peace. All the while, I was conscious of feeling an overwhelming presence—God's presence. But there was another distinct and incredible presence—a presence right in front of me and to my left. It was comforting, stable, honest, and pure. It was all-encompassing. I was not afraid. It was almost like being in the arms of the one you love, when you feel safer being there together. The feeling was different from the bright majesty of light and peace. I had a feeling of someone being close to me. It was comforting and amazing; I felt an indescribable sense of peace and safety, like that of being a child wrapped in his or her mother's arms.

I arrived in a large field, which was green, lush, and bright. It was full of brightness—a marvelous light. I saw myself kneeling before the brightest place. It is indescribable how bright and beautiful it was, but most of all, it was a state of peace beyond your wildest imagination. I had an absolute sense of peace that I will never be able to explain. I know you have read about the marvelous light and peace that transcends all understanding, but I experienced them for real!

I continued to be in awe of the beauty and peace. It was incredible, this overwhelming calmness that I had never before experienced.

I relished just being there—peaceful, secure, and comforted in all the brightness and glory. I remember saying, "I only want to do whatever You want me to do. I promise I'm listening—and please don't hit me so hard next time!" I am now amazed at my complete candor. I was there with all my faults and my goofy sense of humor—right there before the heavens.

There was no sense of time or timing. I have no idea how long I was in this place. I loved lingering in such peace. I was getting the feeling that something was about to change. I said, "I don't really think it is my time to go, but I will if You want. I only have one question: Will my children be okay?" I felt a sense of assurance that they would be and found myself remembering this incredible experience sometime later. You see, things weren't going well here on Earth. My body had been through enough for one week and had begun to shut down.

I believe that through the many faithful prayers chains extending across the country for all of us—my family, my doctors, and me—we all witnessed many miracles and displays of how God was at work during that week.

It took me a long time to tell anyone about this journey. I wasn't sure what to say or how to describe the utter peace I'd felt. I had already experienced being laughed at when I asked for my pain meds by the wrong name so I certainly wasn't going to tell anyone where I had been until months later when it came up in conversation with a friend. She gasped and said, "You left!" Then she proceeded to tell me of other stories she had read that were similar to my description of the meadow, the brilliant light, and the feeling of complete peace beyond explanation.

Here is my personal confirmation of what I felt: *"And the peace of God, which transcends all understanding, will guard your hearts and your minds in Christ Jesus"*. Philippians 4:7 (NIV)

This call came later: *"Whatever you have learned or received or heard from me, or seen in me—put it into practice. And the God of peace will be with you"* Philippians 4:9 (NIV).

I want to express that this is only a glimpse of what awaits. I can't even begin to imagine what heaven will be like when I get to stay!

This time is dear to me. It helps me keep a different perspective on life now. Living according to the Scriptures seems to make more sense. I try to make a conscious effort to give my worries and cares to God. When I can do that, I am free to live as He has purposed for me. Try it, and see what God has in store or you. It might not be without pain or unexpected trials, but I get through them in a better frame of mind, and I always try to be open to see how it all fits together for His glory. It's pretty amazing when you learn to open your mind and heart to live in faith, continually asking for guidance and strength to focus on His will. You will begin to feel what freedom really is. God is love, love is in your heart, open your heart and share God's love.

My father, a veteran, passed away over Memorial Day weekend. Father's Day was just a few weeks away. I received a text message of sympathy from someone who assumed that this must be a tough day after just losing my dad. My response surprised us both. I remember smiling and thinking that Dad was probably experiencing much more than I had. He was finally at peace! No, it wasn't a sad day, not for Dad. He is in a glorious place we can only anticipate. I wanted that for him. It can be tempting to feel sad about the death of a loved one, but please don't. It becomes easier when you think about the peace and joy that those who have passed are now experiencing. I can't wait!

When my children seem to need help or advice, I go back to what I was told, or, more appropriately, what I felt—that they will be okay. I feel a sense of security from this experience, and I think of it often.

My story isn't over. I didn't just walk again, end of story. Well, perhaps it's all in how I choose to interpret that day—whether I choose to dwell on the endless issues, decisions, surgeries, compromises, lost opportunities, and dreams that are no longer dreams or to begin to learn a deeper understanding of God's love.

We should strive to give God the worries of each day so that we can take in the beauty and wonder of His creation. Living life in appreciation and gratitude allows His light to flow through you, bringing a sense of calmness to the craziness of this life. The more this becomes a way of life, the easier it is to sustain. Who knows what the world would be like if we all would take the time to focus on living as God has commanded?

Although there are references to heaven throughout the Bible, none seems to be a complete description of what we will experience. Most are references to heaven being "the great reward," "the crown of life," or "the crown of glory." Revelation has some specific descriptions of the throne in heaven but not of our role in this place.

> *Those whom I love I rebuke and discipline. So be earnest, and repent. Here I am! I stand at the door and knock. If anyone hears my voice and opens the door, I will come in and eat with him, and he with me.* Revelation 3:19–20 (NIV)

> *After this I looked, and there before me was a door standing open in heaven. And the voice I had first heard speaking to me like a trumpet said, "Come up here, and I will show you what must take place after this." At once I was in the Spirit, and there before me was a throne in heaven with someone sitting on it. And the one who sat there had the appearance of jasper and carnelian. A rainbow, resembling an emerald, encircled the throne. Surrounding the throne were twenty-four other thrones, and seated on them were twenty-four elders. They were dressed in white and had crowns of gold on their heads. From the throne came flashes of lightning, rumblings and peals of thunder. Before the throne, seven lamps were blazing. These are the seven spirits of God. Also*

before the throne there was what looked like a sea of glass, clear as crystal.

In the center, around the throne, were four living creatures, and they were covered with eyes, in front and in back. The first living creature was a lion, the second was like an ox, the third had a face like a man, the fourth was like a flying eagle. Each of the four living creatures had six wings and was covered with eyes all around, even under his wings. Day and night they never stop saying:

"Holy, holy, holy
Is the Lord God Almighty,
who was, and is, and is to come." Revelation 4:1–8 (NIV)

I have not stopped giving thanks for you, remembering you in my prayers. I keep asking that the God of our Lord Jesus Christ, the glorious Father, may give you the Spirit of wisdom and revelation so that you may know him better. I pray also that the eyes of your heart may be enlightened in order that you may know the hope to which he has called you, the riches of his glorious inheritance in the saints, and his incomparably great power for us who believe. That power is like the working of his mighty strength, which he exerted in Christ when he raised him from the dead and seated him at his right hand in the heavenly realms, far above all rule and authority, power, and dominion, and every title that can be given, not only in the present age but also in the one to come. And God placed all things under his feet and appointed him to be head over everything for the church, which is his body, the fullness of him who fills everything in every way. Ephesians 1:16–23 (NIV)

Now we know that the earthly tent we live in is destroyed, we have a building from God, an eternal house in heaven, not built by human hands. Meanwhile we groan, longing to be clothed with our heavenly dwelling, because when we are clothed, we will not be found naked. For while we are in this tent, we groan and are burdened, because we do not wish to be unclothed but to be clothed with our heavenly dwelling, so that what is mortal may be swallowed up by life. Now it is God who has made us for this very purpose and has given us the Spirit as a deposit, guaranteeing what is to come. 2 Corinthians 5:1–5 (NIV)

And I know that this man—whether in the body or apart from the body I do not know, but God knows—was caught up in paradise. He heard inexpressible things, things that man is not permitted to tell. 2 Corinthians 12:3–4 (NIV)

Peace I leave with you; my peace I give you. I do not give to you as the world gives. Do not let your hearts be troubled and do not be afraid. John 14:27 (NIV)

When Jesus spoke again to the people, he said, "I am the light of the world. Whoever follows me will never walk in darkness, but will have the light of life." John 8:12 (NIV)

"The kingdom of heaven is like treasure hidden in a field. When a man found it, he hid it again, and then in his joy went and sold all he had and bought the field."

"Again, the kingdom of heaven is like a merchant looking for fine pearls. When he found one of great value, he went away and sold everything he had and bought it." Matthew 13:44–45 (NIV)

In my Father's house are many rooms; if it were not so, I would have told you. I am going there to prepare a place for you. And if I go and prepare a place for you, I will come back and take you to be with me that you also may be where I am. You know the way to the place where I am going. John 14:2–4 (NIV)

For you were once darkness, but now you are light in the Lord. Live as children of light (for the fruit of the light consists in all goodness, righteousness and truth) and find out what pleases the Lord. Ephesians 5:8–10 (NIV)

There is no complete description in the Bible of what heaven is like. I believe that is because heaven is beyond our human ability to comprehend. Those who have had a glimpse of what awaits mostly describe the feelings. Only a rare few have crossed over to heaven and been allowed to return, giving us a more concrete physical description of heaven or of God Himself.

The following Scripture passages are among the few that describe heaven as a place.

This is the message we have heard from him and declare to you: God is light; in him there is no darkness at all. 1 John 1:5 (NIV)

*The people walking in darkness
have seen a great light;
on those living in the land of the shadow of death
a light has dawned.* Isaiah 9:2 (NIV)

Then I saw a new heaven and a new earth, for the first heaven and the first earth had passed away, and there was no longer any sea. I saw the Holy City, the new Jerusalem, coming down out of heaven from God, prepared as a bride beautifully dressed for her husband. And I heard a loud voice from the throne saying, "Now the dwelling of God is with men, and he will live with them. They will be his people, and God himself will be with them and be their God. He will wipe every tear from their eyes. There will be no more death or mourning or crying or pain, for the order of things has passed away."

He who was seated on the throne said, "I am making everything new!" Then he said, "Write this down for these words are trustworthy and true."

One of the seven angels who had the seven bowls full of the seven last plaques came and said to me, "Come, I will show you the bride, the wife of the Lamb." And he carried me away in the Spirit to a mountain great and high, and showed me the Holy City, Jerusalem, coming down out of heaven from God. It shone with the glory of God, and its brilliance was like that of a very precious jewel, like a jasper, clear as crystal. It had a great, high wall with twelve gates, and with twelve angels at the gates. On the gates were written the names of the twelve tribes of Israel. There were three gates on the east, three on the north, three on the south and three on the west. The wall of the city had twelve foundations and on them were the names of the twelve apostles of the Lamb.

The angel who talked with me had a measuring rod of gold to measure the city, its gates and its walls. The city was laid out like a square, as long as it was wide. He measured the city with the rod and found it to be 12,000 stadia in length, and as wide and high as it is long. He measured its wall and it was 144 cubits thick, by man's measurement, which the angel was using. The wall was made of jasper, and the city of pure gold, as pure as glass. The foundations of the city walls were decorated with every kind of precious stone. The first foundation was jasper, the second was sapphire, the third chalcedony, the fourth emerald, the fifth sardonyx, the sixth carnelian, the seventh chrysolite, the eighth beryl, the ninth topaz, the tenth chrysoprase, the eleventh jacinth, and the twelfth amethyst. The twelve gates were twelve pearls, each gate made of a single pearl. The great street of the city was pure gold, like transparent glass.

I did not see a temple in the city, because the Lord God Almighty and the Lamb are its temple. The city does not need the sun or the moon to shine on it, for the glory of God gives it light, and the Lamb is its lamp. The nations will walk by its light, and the kings of the earth will bring their splendor into it. On no day will its gates ever be shut, for there will be no night there. The glory and honor of the nations will be brought onto it. Nothing impure will ever enter it, nor will anyone who does what is shameful or deceitful but only those whose names are written in the Lamb's book of life. Revelation 21:1–5; 9:27 (NIV)

Then the angel showed me the river of the water of life, as clear as crystal, flowing from the throne of God and of the Lamb down the middle of the great street of the city. On each side of the river stood the tree of life, bearing twelve crops of fruit, yielding its fruit every month. And the leaves of the tree are for the healing of the nations. No longer will there be any curse. The throne of God and the Lamb will be in the city, and his servants will serve him. They will see his face, and his name will be on their foreheads. There will be no more night. They will not need the light of a lamp or the light of the sun, for the Lord God will give them light. And they will reign for ever and ever.

> *The angel said to me, "These words are trustworthy and true. The Lord, the God of the spirits of the prophets, sent his angel to show his servants the things that must soon take place."*
> Revelation 22:1–6 (NIV)

It seems we will all have to wait until our appointed day to experience heaven fully. But this glimpse is enough to make me no longer fear death but embrace life each day and look with anticipation to what awaits!

8

MOMENT TO MOMENT

"The people you live among will see how awesome
is the work that I, the Lord, will do for you."
~Exodus 34:10b (NIV)

"For I know the plans I have for you," declares the LORD, "plans to prosper you and not to harm you, plans to give you hope and a future". Jeremiah 29:11 (NIV)—I held on to this idea tightly. I knew I would walk again someday. I was not sure whether it would be on my own legs or when it would happen, but I *would* walk, and I didn't want to think about what might happen in the meantime.

Deep in my heart, I held close the belief that I was blessed. *That's it—I am blessed!* I clung to that thought and that thought alone. I didn't dwell on what I didn't have. Actually, my attorney asked me to write down what it took to live each day. I was upset by that request, because I knew that what people really wanted to know was what I could not do, what I had lost. I was not going to take time out of my day to reflect on what I didn't have. I believed within my heart that my recovery would be lifelong, so I was not going to set more personal goals for some specific ability and potentially set myself up for more heartache in the event I didn't achieve something in my own time frame. See how easy it is to get off track!

Our focus should always be on giving our struggles to God. We know He will handle things in His own time. I was simply living that out. Again, He allowed me to live in each moment, not to set goals that would bring more heartache. I wasn't going to waste what energy I did have. I knew I was blessed. I kept thankfulness and joy in my heart, which allowed me to stay out of the rut life can become. I lived, from the moment I was trapped in the car and heard the paramedics say, "We're running out of time," to celebrate each and every little movement I could improve on or each task I could accomplish. In the back of my mind, I knew there could always be a tradeoff or, as time passed and other effects were revealed, there could be something that would need surgical attention. I consider this another huge blessing, not to have spent my time and energy on loss. God never allowed me to go there. Sure, I occasionally had moments of tears and anticipation of when it would all end, but those were short lived.

One evening, my husband wheeled me outside, and then he went back inside to get something. At that moment, I was overcome with the enormity of the accident. My kids were hurting, and so were friends, family, neighbors, and my church family. Would I ever walk again? Would I ever work again? What about the cost of all of this? This was too much to bear. I decided to give up. After about three seconds, I started to laugh. The truth was, I didn't know how to give up! God didn't let me linger in the pits too long. I had come to know that I needed to believe in His divine plan.

I was looking over some things that I wrote in December 2006. By then, I was up and walking on both legs. I would still periodically experience a sharp, cutting pain in my shoulder. I could drive, however. Every moment, though, was different. I did not live with progress from one level of accomplishment to another. There was not a clear step of recovery at any point. There would always be cautions as I gained some movement or flexibility. Balance was always a concern. I needed to remain balanced because I could not afford to fall. I not only had lost my normally quick reflexes to catch or stop a fall but also didn't have any body parts to rely on during a fall. I was aware of the potential repercussions. There were unending possibilities of what could happen if I were to fall. I hope you can see that all of the moments, some more traumatic and tearful than others, had silver linings and glory to cherish in my heart.

Recently, I was invited to be a staff member at a retreat. I was also asked to lead a small group for the weekend and present one of the lessons or talks to the larger assembly. It was my call to action. After being there for several days with these people I had never met, I formed a strong bond with them on many levels. I loved being a part of the small group as we shared what each speaker had to say and what it meant to each of us. It was a great dynamic, as we had men and women of all ages, backgrounds, and stages in life. One gentleman shared with me how he took notes as each speaker presented. He had a system in his note-taking that would help him remember what touched him the most. If the speaker made a point he wanted to remember, he would put a square around the note. If the lesson was something that really hit home, he would mark it with two squares. After my presentation, he was touched and proud, as I was his group leader, and he put three squares in his notebook! It might not sound like a lot to you, but to realize I had impacted someone that deeply was beyond words to me. We all shared a lot that weekend, but I hold that moment close to my heart. I lived that weekend in total vulnerability. I felt such closeness with Christ in the ability to not only share my story but also listen as others shared their stories and feelings. Being a small part of His greater work is indeed humbling.

In preparing for that weekend, I prayed for guidance, wrote the presentation, and left it alone. When I reread it, I didn't change much. I learned from what God had allowed me to write. God is love, love is in your heart open your heart, and share God's love. It is the simple things in life that bring the greatest joy. I quoted lines from my favorite song, "Testify to Love," which has impacted my life greatly: "Through every word of every story, speak what God has done."

In sharing some moments that live in my heart as true glory, I'd like to share one of my favorite books, *The Power of a Whisper*, by Bill Hybels. I read this book in a small-group setting. Each week, my group watched the DVD while Bill Hybels discussed his experiences. I immediately connected with what he had to say and who he seemed to be. As I dove into the book, I highlighted what seemed to be the entire book!

Let me share a quote from his book that verbalizes what I could not. He attributes this newfound mental and spiritual clarity to the fact that God divinely orchestrated this entire series of miraculous steps. "God blessed us to be a blessing," he says. "This story isn't about two men as much as it's about our wonder-working God."

This is my intent as well. I never wanted this book to be about me, but I feel like I am here to share what I have seen and felt so that others might see that "it's about our wonder-working God."

Shortly after I finished reading *The Power of a Whisper* the first time, I was relaxing early one morning. I sat in quiet amazement of my surroundings. I was recently divorced, so life was upside down, to say the least. While there was much to worry about, I was trying not to live in fear but, rather, to rest in God's grace. As things came to my mind, I reached for a pen and started writing. I wrote about what you can see in a moment—the picture.

What you see in any given moment can depend entirely on what's in your heart. Sunday morning, I awoke early and sat in my rocker with a nice, hot cup of coffee and every intention of reading. Eventually, with a feeling of great peace, I drifted from my book to looking around my home, which is full of signs of all that has transpired over the years. I sat in solitude, waiting and listening intently for God's whisper.

I was entrenched in taking in my home. Out of the fury of a broken marriage came peace and a place of solitude for me as well as for our family and friends, old and new.

As I looked around, I glanced at a large painting. It's wonderful! I normally would not have ventured to spend that kind of money on a painting. I never had before, but it completes our home. It is a place I want to go—a dream, really—probably in Greece or Italy. There's a quaint bungalow surrounded by a variety of beautiful flowers and a view of a lake. I looked beneath the picture to see the angel my son had given me that Christmas; its wings of copper shone in the morning light. It is a gift of hope and acknowledgment of the angels that are ever present in our lives. It is a reminder of God's love and light, always shining, leading the way.

Next to the angel, I looked at the flowers my daughter and I bought. We bought them during a storm of life. I have them only until she has a place for them. Until then, we share in their hope and beauty. They are white roses—pure and full of hope. On the other side, I observed the candle that was with me in the car that overturned and changed my life. My son found it, still intact through it all, as I know I will be too.

"In all things God works for the good of those who love Him, who have been called according to His purpose". Romans 8:28 (NIV) When I read this verse, I am reminded that He asks us to take time to listen quietly to His whispers.

Here is a special moment that is, in fact, a glory—a mom listening to her child's heartache but seeing that it had served a noble purpose. This is what my daughter wrote on her med-school application four years after the accident:

> *During this time, I also witnessed medicine from a completely different vantage point: that of a frightened 18-year-old afraid of losing her mother. The result of a horrendous collision, my mother's injuries were catastrophic and the treatments touch-and-go. The healing process was a long and arduous journey, one that involved many physicians. The good ones explained what they did and why, in addition to answering our questions. Others treated my mother as though she was unimportant and condescendingly dismissed our fears. This perspective provided me with invaluable insight into the lives of patients and their loved ones. First-hand knowledge of their fears and challenges that I carry with me to this day.*

I try to remember things like this. Kami always seemed to be destined to become a doctor. But now more than ever, I am confident that she will treat her patients with compassion like no other.

The impact my accident and the aftermath had on my children and family is obvious, but realizing the impact my experience has had on others amazes me. Over the years, I have been able to meet some of my rescue workers. They too were deeply affected. Many people from my church still stop me for quiet moments to comment on what a miracle it is that I am walking. My church family was right there, many even at the scene, praying, and the prayers were unending. Most people don't understand the depth of physical destruction—and that's okay with me. I'd much rather have them focus on what God has done and realize it was done through their prayers. I feel as if I am a piece of God's creation on display for all to see. It wasn't I who got through this; it was God performing many miracles to get me where I am today. Now I eagerly share these experiences of what God has promised to *"see how awesome is the work that I, the LORD, will do for you."* Exodus 34:10b (NIV)

Some of the memories still bring tears, but mostly, they bring amazement and lots of laughter. I told my kids early on that we would laugh through this experience—and we did! We often remember the little things. My daughter was laughing recently because I had sent her a picture of my shoes the day I was allowed to walk on both legs. She wasn't sure what the picture was. So naturally, I am sending her one right now as I write this. I had surgery on my left foot a few months ago and have been wearing the attractive little black boot. Today I have on a pair—yes, *pair*—of little white Keds. So I'll share this milestone with her via text message!

I pray that as you begin to give Him your worries, you too will open your hearts to see each moment for the glory it is. Rest in the knowledge that God is right there beside you. Verse after verse in the Bible promises us His presence, even through the tough times—maybe *especially* in the tough times.

Some are specific to a time and place, yet another example of how He keeps His promise to protect. Other times, He speaks to us to remember that He is there. See how many times He reminds us when we take the time to read His Word.

"There's only one way to infuse our belief in Jesus with genuine truth and healing power: living moment by moment with Him, allowing His Spirit to lead us and align our hearts with Christ alone." Charles Stanley, "Heart Language Reclaiming Christian Vocabulary", In-Touch, January 2013,53.

9

GLORY TO GLORY

"My eyes are ever on the Lord, for only he will
release my feet from the snare."
~Psalm 25:15 (NIV)

You can image how thrilled I was to be alive. I actually didn't think of it in those terms. It was more as if I felt gratitude and wonder in each moment, and I was thankful that this was where I lived. But the next gift, although I never doubted it in my heart, was glorious to experience.

When my orthopedic surgeon decided to allow me to be weight bearing on both legs, he was sweet. He was trying to stress what he wanted me to do but seemed as if he did not want to put too much pressure on me. I felt he was not sure I would be able to do what he asked.

He gave me a walker—you know, the ugly steel-looking thing. He was specific, addressing me almost as if I were a child, but in a caring and not a demeaning way. He told me he wanted me to *try* to walk with the walker. He wanted to see me back in thirty days. I laughed to myself. Of course I would be walking in thirty days. I was not given the option but the order to walk!

The walker was awful. Remember, my left shoulder had been broken. It was actually more painful than my legs most of the time. Using a walker and depending heavily on my shoulders was far more difficult than putting weight on both legs. I could quickly see that I had to make a conscious decision to use the walker—but I did!

For three days, I tried hard to use the walker instead of the wheelchair, but it was terribly awkward. The painful shoulder made me hesitant. Of course, I was afraid I might fall, even though I did not feel unsteady.

On August 24, 2006, I got up and ready to try walking with my new equipment. Each moment was a learning experience, just being upright instead of in the wheelchair. By now, you have probably figured out that I felt as if this new device was getting me nowhere. It was cumbersome, awkward, and, frankly, annoying to use this walker. So I stood next to the island in the kitchen, holding on to the countertop. I took a step and then another step and continued to be amazed that nothing hurt or even felt awkward. Just knowing I was standing on two legs—*my* two legs—was like flying. It was unbelievable! I continued cautiously to take a step at a time, holding on to the countertop. Eventually, I made it around the entire island! I think I must have been in a state of shock. I was so excited, but how could I tell somebody? I did it again, slowly and cautiously, and then, miraculously, several more times. Well, by this time, I just had to tell someone! I knew no one would believe me. I remember calling my husband at work. He didn't answer, so I left him a rather tearful and probably almost incoherent message, crying and anxious to tell him, "I am walking! I am really walking! I know you won't believe me, but I am up and walking by myself!"

I was terribly disappointed that there I was, standing in my kitchen on my own legs, walking around the island, and I was all by myself. But Matt wasn't answering. I tried to be patient. It felt like hours had gone by, so I called him again. My message was tearful and excited at the same time: "I know you won't believe me, but I am walking by myself!"

I decided I simply *had* to share this moment with someone, so I called Kathie, my friend and neighbor. She had been by my side to help me, and she had been there for the entire family through all of this. We left the front door unlocked in those days so that she could get into the house, because the front door was raised a step. I could not get there to open it.

I can't imagine what Kathie must have thought when she listened to the message I left. She came over in just a few short minutes. The front door flew open, and Kathie screamed my name to see if I was all right. I said, "I'm up here." I was standing at the top of the stairs. I now don't remember how or why I chose to attempt climbing the stairs, but I did. I suspect I went up the stairs on my behind, as I had been doing for several months, but it was exciting to see Kathie from upstairs. She ran up to give me a hug.

Somehow, we got downstairs. Then my husband called. He had understood my message! He said that he was heading home. Slowly and carefully, Kathie walked me down the driveway. That was a feat in itself, since the driveway is pretty steep, but nothing mattered.

I was walking on my own legs, sharing the moment with a dear friend who had been with me through all the pain, uncertainty, and upheaval in the family.

We made it down to the cul-de-sac. Kathie, the other women who lived on the cul-de-sac, and I had spent many hours there. Often, our husbands would call out remarks about dinner being later! After a long day, it was nice to catch up with the ladies.

So there we were, standing in that same cul-de-sac together, thinking about how long it had been since we'd stood together and remembering how often at least one of the husbands would yell out the window.

Then Matt came flying around the corner. He came close enough for a quick word, and then he said, "Stay there. I'm going to go back up to the end of the street so you can walk to me!"

It was one of the most touching moments. The last five months now appeared as a flash in time. To have been through all of this—the rescue, paramedics, firefighters, ICU, doctors, prayer teams, cards, calls, dinners, and encouragement for us all and now, here it was—the moment of glory I never *really* had thought about! Although I had known I would walk again, I had never stopped to think about what it would actually be like.

And so another leg of the journey began—no pun intended. I slowly and carefully walked down the street to my husband while Kathie looked on. It was as if time had stopped. For me, it is a memory and feeling that will remain forever. I was living out a miracle, a gift that no one can deny.

Later that afternoon, I heard my son's car pulling in the driveway. I slowly and carefully got up and stood at the back hallway. Trey walked in, said hi, and then halted as suddenly as if stopped by an army. "You're walking," he said in disbelief.

And so the journey continues as I face the trials and successes of my newfound gift, the gift of walking on my own legs. Even though the legs are mine physically, they feel as if they are foreign attachments. I welcome them but live in awareness that they are a gift I hold with great pride and reverence in the acknowledgment of what He has done.

"As you persevere along the path I have prepared for you, depending on My strength to sustain you, expect to see miracles—and you will. Miracles are not always visible to the naked eye, but those who *live by faith* can see them clearly. *Living by faith, rather than sight,* enables you to see My Glory." Sarah Young, Jesus Calling:Enjoying Peace in His Presence,(Thomas Nelson 2004) 372

Below is a passage that is so direct yet broad, vast and yet specific of what God wants us to do and what He will do for us.

> *Rejoice in the Lord always. I will say it again: Rejoice! Let your gentleness be evident to all. The Lord is near. Do not be anxious about anything, but in everything, by prayer and petition, with thanksgiving, present your requests to God. And the peace of God, which transcends all understanding, will guard your hearts and your minds in Christ Jesus.*
>
> *Finally brothers, whatever is true, whatever is noble, whatever is right, whatever is pure, whatever is lovely, whatever is admirable—if anything is excellent or praiseworthy—think about such things. Whatever you have learned or received or heard from me, or seen in me—put into practice. And the God of peace will be with you.* Philippians 4:4–13 (NIV)

This passage encompasses so much of what transpired in those five short months. I am thankful to all whom I can mention by name and to those I can't. My entire family was surrounded in prayer, and even in difficult moments or moments of human emotion, we were somehow almost shielded from living in that hurt. We lived knowing God would bring us through, whatever that was to look like.

My story is personal to me, but somehow, through my telling these stories, people respond in awe. The response should not be awe—God commands us to live in faith, prayer, patience, comfort, and peace. I never intended to live out an example of giving one's life over to God, but this was somehow exactly what happened. I believe it might have been because I was so incapacitated—not only physically but also, because of the medications, mentally—that I turned to what I knew in my heart. Everything was in God's hands, no doubt, and that reassurance was where my heart rested. It's kind of funny—this is exactly what dying to yourself and living in God means, but I'd never really understood it before.

> *Then he said to them all: "If anyone would come after me, he must deny himself and take up his cross daily and follow me. For whoever wants to save his life will lose it, but whoever loses his life for me will save it. What good is it for a man to gain the whole world, and yet lose or forfeit his very self? If anyone is ashamed of me and my words, the Son of Man will be ashamed of him when he comes in his glory and in the glory of the Father and of the holy angels. I tell you the truth, some who are standing here will not taste death before they see the kingdom of God."* Luke 9:23–27 (NIV)
>
> *Humble yourselves, therefore, under God's mighty hand, that he may lift you up in due time. Cast all your anxiety on him because he cares for you.*
>
> *Be self-controlled and alert. Your enemy the devil prowls around like a roaring lion looking for someone to devour. Resist him, standing firm in the faith, because you know that your brothers throughout the world are undergoing the same kind of suffering.*
>
> *And the God of all grace, who called you to his eternal glory in Christ, after you have suffered a little while, will himself restore you and make you strong, firm and steadfast. To him be the power for ever and ever. Amen.* 1 Peter 5:6–11 (NIV)

Many times, much to the dismay of others, I was not going to worry. I couldn't. My brain was focused on every movement and on the desperation of wanting to shield my children and wanting them to have a normal life. I was not convinced that *normal* would ever be a word I would use again. And I will not, but it's with great delight that I can say nothing is normal!

Life has changed for many since that day—my family, first and foremost. I know for a fact that some of the rescue teams from that day see God's hand clearly. People from my church still stop me in quiet moments to recall the miracle of my ability to walk, and others have witnessed this miracle. Some of these I have come to know years after the accident. People remember praying for everyone involved in the accident that day, never knowing the names of the individuals they were praying for. Thank you!

Below is a Scripture passage I would like you to ponder. Give yourself credit for things you *have* done in faith. It will help you make the decision to make the conscious effort to give your burdens to Him and walk in faith.

> *Now faith is being sure of what we hope for and certain of what we do not see. This is what the ancients were commended for.*
>
> *By faith we understand that the universe was formed at God's command, so that what is seen was not made out of what was visible.*
>
> *By faith Abel offered God a better sacrifice than Cain did. By faith he was commended as a righteous man, when God spoke well of his offerings. And by faith he still speaks, even though he is dead.*
>
> *By faith Enoch was taken from this life, so that he did not experience death; he could not be found, because God*

had taken him away. For before he was taken, he was commended as one who pleased God. And without faith it is impossible to please God, because anyone who comes to him must believe that he exists and that he rewards those who earnestly seek him.

By faith Noah, when warned about things not yet seen, in holy fear built an ark to save his family. By his faith he condemned the world and became heir of the righteousness that comes from faith.

By faith Abraham, when called to go to a place he would later receive as his inheritance, obeyed and went, even though he did not know where he was going. By faith he made his home in the promised land like a stranger in a foreign country; he lived in tents, as did Isaac and Jacob, who were heirs with him of the same promise. For he was looking forward to the city with foundations, whose architect and builder is God.

By faith Abraham, even though he was past age—and Sarah herself was barren—was enabled to become a father because he considered him faithful who had made the promise. And so from this one man, and he as good as dead, came descendants as numerous as the stars in the sky and as countless ad the sand on the seashore.

All these people were still living by faith when they died. They did not receive the things promised; they only saw them and welcomed them from a distance. And they admitted that they were aliens and strangers on earth. People who say such things show that they are looking for a country of their own. If they had been thinking of the country they had left, they would have had opportunity to return. Instead, they were longing for a better country—a heavenly one. Therefore God is not ashamed to be called their God, for he has prepared a city for them.

By faith Abraham, when God tested him, offered Isaac as a sacrifice. He who had received promises was about to sacrifice his one and only son, even though God had said to him, "It is through Isaac that your offspring will be reckoned." Abraham reasoned that God could raise the dead, and figuratively speaking, he did receive Isaac back from death.

By faith Isaac blessed Jacob and Esau in regard to their future.

By faith Jacob, when he was dying, blessed each of Joseph's sons and worshiped as he leaned on the top of his staff.

By faith Joseph, when his end was near, spoke about the exodus of the Israelites from Egypt and gave instructions about his bones.

By faith Moses' parents hid him for three months after he was born, because they saw he was no ordinary child, and they were not afraid of the king's edict.

By faith Moses, when he had grown up, refused to be known as the son of the Pharaoh's daughter. He chose to be mistreated along with the people of God rather than to enjoy the pleasures of sin for a short time. He regarded disgrace for the sake of Christ as of greater value than the treasures of Egypt, because he was looking ahead to his reward. By faith he left Egypt, not fearing the king's anger; he persevered because he saw him who is invisible. By faith he kept the Passover and the sprinkling of blood, so that the destroyer of the firstborn would not touch the firstborn of Israel.

By faith the people passed through the Red Sea as on dry land; but when the Egyptians tried to do so, they were drowned.

By faith the walls of Jericho fell, after the people had marched around them for seven days.

By faith the prostitute Rahab, because she welcomed the spies, was not killed with those who were disobedient.

And what more shall I say? I do not have time to tell about Gideon, Barak, Samson, Jephthah, David, Samuel and the prophets, who through faith conquered kingdoms, administered justice, and gained what was promised; who shut the mouths of lions, quenched the fury of the flames, and escaped the edge of the sword; whose weakness was turned into strength; and who became powerful in battle and routed foreign armies. Women received back their dead, raised to life again. Others were tortured and refused to be released, so that they might gain a better resurrection. Some faced jeers and flogging, while still others were chained and put in prison. They were stoned; they were sawed in two; they were put to death by the sword. They went about in sheepskins and goatskins, destitute, persecuted and mistreated—the world was not worthy of them. They wandered in deserts and mountains, and in caves and holes in the ground.

These were all commended for their faith. Yet none of them received what had been promised. God had planned something better for us that only together with us would they be made perfect. Hebrews 11:1–39 (NIV)

GOD'S GRACE CONTINUES

In 2008, I had another reconstructive surgery. During my physical therapy, someone asked if I was going to run in the Houston Marathon. That was not an option, but the question got me thinking. So in January of 2009, I did walk the Houston Half Marathon and completed it in three hours and twenty-three minutes! God's grace continues.

My daughter, Kami, graduated from the University of Texas at San Antonio and married last year. She just graduated from the University of Texas Medical Branch in Galveston, Texas, and has joined the staff at John's Hopkins in pediatrics.

My son, Trey, graduated from high school and went on to graduate from Texas A&M University. He is currently working for a large oil company.

Then there is Judy Armstrong's story. During our journey together, while editing this book, she experienced some health issues that resulted in her own near-death experience. It was obvious that God's hand was upon both of us on more than one occasion.

And, of course, the stories continue. What a joy it is to meet people who ask to hear my stories and then eagerly share their stories with me. Hearing how God has blessed them is still amazing to me. It warms my heart.

Where is God leading you?

Made in the USA
Middletown, DE
14 November 2014